Dear Readers:

SURVIVAL may not be an easy book to read, for it portrays all too vividly the tragedy of crime among ordinary people. But because it teaches you how to protect yourself, it is essential to read it and use it.

Hugh C. McDonald doesn't tell you to turn your home into an armed fort. He won't teach you martial arts. SURVIVAL is *not* about the sociological problems of crime and criminal justice, or a polemic about vengeance.

Instead, it is simply a set of commonsense tactics and survival strategies, based on true incidents, for attempting to control your own *and* someone else's behavior in a high-intensity situation. By preparing *in advance*, you'll be in a much better position to avoid panic and save yourself from murder, rape, a mugging, or a robbery. In the long run, SURVIVAL can help to save *all* of us—victim, perpetrator, and public—from the humiliation of crime.

We're publishing SURVIVAL to share Hugh C. McDonald's forty years of experience protecting the public. We feel it could be one of the most important books you'll ever buy.

Ballantine Books

Survival

Hugh C. McDonald

BALLANTINE BOOKS • NEW YORK

Library of Congress Catalog Card Number: 81-066655

ISBN 0-345-29735-0

Manufactured in the United States of America

First Ballantine Books Edition: January 1982

9 8 7 6 5 4 3 2 1

Cover photo © 1981 by Tony Korody

About Hugh C. McDonald

In the late spring of 1942, a small group of men met at a banquet room in New York's La Guardia Airport. Each one belonged to what is probably the most distinguished and select club in the world: "To Kill or Be Killed." They had gathered around a bare wooden table to drink a toast and pay their respects to Lieutenant Hugh C. McDonald, their first elected president and the man who had spent months training them in the art of survival and attack. Thus began a brilliant career of service lasting over thirty years.

Shortly after Secretary of the Navy James Forrestal fell to his death from a hospital window in the Washington, D.C., area, the Central Intelligence Agency contracted a man and employed him to investigate the circumstances leading to the secretary's death. The final report revealed a probability that Mr. Forrestal had not committed suicide as had been generally reported but rather was the victim of a sophisticated technique of audio-sublimation suggestion. That investigator was Hugh C. McDonald.

These incidents took place over a span of twenty-seven years, during which time Mr. McDonald was a member of the Los Angeles County Sheriff's Department. Starting from the position of deputy sheriff, he rose to the rank of division chief in the fifth-largest law enforcement agency in America. He distinguished himself in his chosen profession and is widely known for his contribution of the "Identi-Kit," the "Identicator," and other systems currently used by law enforcement agencies throughout the world. McDonald has been a member of the staff of the University of California at Los Angeles, the University of Southern California, the University of Oklahoma, and the University of Louisville. His books—*The Investigation of Sex Crimes, The Classification of Police Photographs,* and *The Psychology of Police Interrogation*—are standard texts in police academies throughout the world.

Mr. McDonald, whose final assignment in the Sheriff's Department placed him in command of six hundred detective sergeants, is a graduate of the sixty-seventh class of the FBI Academy in Washington, D.C. In the course of his distinguished career, McDonald has undertaken a great many special assignments, including being chief of security for Senator Barry Goldwater's presidential campaign. That was the year after the assassination of President John F. Kennedy and fears were running high. In the words of Dean Burch, the national chairman of the Republican party, they wanted the best available. They got him.

Survival

PROLOGUE

Four hundred miles east of Hawaii, low over the ocean, a DC-6 pilot fought successfully to keep panic out of his voice. "Ladies and gentlemen, we will strike the ocean's surface in a normal landing attitude. The aircraft's wheels will be in a retracted position; you will feel two severe jolts as our plane settles onto the surface. Have your life jackets on, ready for inflation when flight attendants tell you to inflate. Good luck." One hundred and three passengers remained alive and were rescued shortly after the plane ditched. Their lives were saved because each of them wore a life jacket that kept him or her afloat until help arrived.

1944. Somewhere in London. Air-raid sirens filled the night with their mournful wail. Thousands of men, women, and children left warm beds and trudged in orderly fashion to predesignated air-raid shelters. Hundreds died, but thousands lived because they had been instructed in what to do before enemy bombers dropped their deadly cargo.

1964. A United States Navy submarine settled to the ocean floor somewhere off the north Atlantic coast. More than three hundred men trapped in the mortally wounded vessel remained calm. There was no sign of panic. Each man went about his business of preparing for evacuation. Well trained in the use of sophisticated equipment, all were saved. Panic was averted and rescue made possible by thoughtful and precise training on how to handle a potentially deadly circumstance.

For those who read it, *Survival* will be their life jacket, their shelter against attack, and finally their source of knowledge about how to avoid panic—that state of mind which leads to chaos and death during trying circumstances.

Survival readers will be prepared to avoid circumstances which lead to tragedy because they can recognize the face of danger. If, however, disaster strikes without warning, they will be capable of meeting the test and surviving where others might die.

It has been said by many who have read *Survival* that it will save thousands of lives. One of those lives might be yours. The violence and aggression that is rife in America now afflicts every country in the world. No one can escape, and therefore everyone must learn to live by following a set of rules that will offer protection and even immunization against the effects of violence.

It is to this purpose that the author of *Survival* dedicates his work. Those who read this book and understand its meaning and purpose will not be overwhelmed by a sense of hopelessness. Rather they will be buoyed by a sense of joy and confidence. Joy for the chance to live in America and meet its challenge, and confidence in their ability to exist without undue fear, thus accomplishing personal goals.

1

Holly Monihan glanced at a round-faced clock built into the tan brick wall. It showed ten minutes to five.

Holly worked as a clerk typist in a large room with twenty other young women. Each had a small desk and modern electric typewriter; all were expert at their business. Over eighty words per minute without error. As employees of a large insurance company, they typed claims and counterclaims seven hours each workday. For her expertise each woman took home $250 per week and in addition was given excellent medical coverage, including dental care.

Holly stretched, pulled the long legal paper from her typewriter, and began to put things away. At five o'clock she was free to go. It was Friday night, and although she didn't have a date, Holly looked forward to spending a few hours at her favorite disco bar just outside the city limits of Evanston, Illinois, a bedroom community in suburban Chicago. She lived alone on the third floor of a modern, comfortable apartment complex. The bar was outside the Evanston city limits because no establishment within those limits was allowed to serve alcoholic beverages.

"Are you going to the Music Shop tonight, Holly?" Antoinette Gatts called from two desks away.

"Toni, you know I go there every Friday night. It's a big thing for me. Will I see you there?"

Toni's big brown eyes sparkled. "Sure, but I thought we might go out to your place for dinner, and then if things didn't work out I could spend the night with you. That's only a few blocks from the Shop; it's an easy walk if we don't connect."

"Great! We'll catch the five forty and get to my place before six thirty. Did you bring a change with you this morning?" Holly, in contrast to the dark-complexioned Antoinette, was a blue-eyed natural blonde. In their late twenties, both young women worked hard at being attractive and succeeded even beyond their hopes.

Antoinette and Holly had known each other for more than a year and felt comfortable both double-dating and going their own ways. When the latter happened, they made it a practice to retire to the ladies' room and discuss their prospective dates. They avoided "kinky" attachments and sought each other's advice before making a commitment that would separate them for the night.

It was the middle of June and hot. The young women were dressed in jeans and summer blouses. The Music Shop crowd were all young, mostly casual acquaintances. Music was loud with a frantic beat, which kept the young people swaying, bouncing, touching, then parting, sweating but not uncomfortable as the throbbing sounds floated them like a curling ocean wave into a dreamy oblivion.

It was after midnight, and Holly and Toni had already talked about the dark-haired young man who wanted to take Toni home. They had decided it would be all right, so Toni split with her date, leaving Holly to fend for herself.

It may have been the oppressive heat, or maybe the day at the office had been particularly difficult. For whatever reason, Holly Monihan did not feel up to the game and

4

decided she would walk the few short blocks to her apartment alone. No one had seemed very interested in her, and she was not nervous. It was after 1:30 a.m.

Holly entered her third-floor apartment. A table lamp, which she always turned on when leaving, cast a soft glow. Because it was hot, Holly had left open a sliding glass door leading onto a small balcony. The cooling breeze billowed her lace curtains and felt good. She walked into her bedroom and switched on the light.

Holly recoiled in terror. The room was a mess. Everything was turned upside down. Someone had ransacked her room. She turned and moved back into the sitting room. There was a phone on the counter top that separated her living room from a small kitchen.

As she reached for the phone a man's voice ordered, "Don't touch that phone!"

Holly spun around. The man stood in the open balcony door and must have been there when Holly entered the apartment. She tried to keep panic out of her voice. "Who are you and what do you want?" she demanded.

The man moved toward her. He was big, over six feet tall, and dirty-looking.

Holly sensed danger and backed away. "There's nothing of any value here. Why don't you just leave?" Her voice was trembling.

He struck like a cat. There was no sound. His first blow sent Holly reeling into the kitchen counter. In desperation she picked up a food processor and struck back at him.

It glanced off his face. He growled like an animal.

Holly Monihan, beaten and raped repeatedly, died many times that night before her heart stopped. The investigator's report stated she had put up a fierce fight, but the savage attack gave her no chance to survive.

5

Survival Techniques and Analysis

Holly Monihan Case

Following each case history, the "Survival Techniques and Analysis" *section will answer questions raised by the details of each situation and point out how to avoid the circumstances that led to danger and tragedy.*

Many young women in America have a life-style similar to Holly Monihan's. Most of them manage to survive without meeting circumstances that result in murder and rape. Holly's nightmare was not the result of any one specific act or error on her part. A series of attitudes and circumstances are involved.

If Holly had understood and recognized the dangers that exist in her "concrete jungle," she could have avoided setting up an opportunity for those dangers to close in. This is not to say that Holly should have lived her life in an atmosphere of constant fear. Young women like Holly *can* live happy, useful, and productive lives without being bugged to death by fear syndromes. They *can* go out at night and enjoy doing all the things young people have enjoyed doing since the beginning of time. There is no need for them to meet Holly's fate.

Let's take a careful look at Holly's case and see what led to her death. There is an indication that Holly was not fully aware of the dangers that surrounded her and had become careless about personal safety. This can happen with incredible ease. The pattern of uneventful day-to-day routine causes senses to become dulled. It is interesting that Holly and Toni took precautions to evaluate any pending date they met at the Music Shop. On the other hand, Holly apparently gave no thought to the dangers of walking home alone at 1:30 a.m. Even a short walk in the Evanston/ Chicago area or in any other area would be a dangerous exposure.

While it's true that the walk home didn't cause Holly's problem, the same casual neglect resulted in her ignoring commonsense precautions and ultimately led to her death. That evening when she left the window of her third-floor apartment open, it was an invitation to the cat burglar. What really happened was that Holly surprised a burglar. She walked in on him and became a rape and murder victim by accident. The burglar had no intention of committing those acts when he entered her apartment. But when Holly surprised him, she became a target of opportunity—young, pretty, and alone.

Even after an intruder entered through the open window, Holly might have saved her life. First, when she walked into her bedroom and realized someone had been there, she should have run out of the apartment instantly. She moved toward the telephone, an act that kept her in the apartment and made her easy prey for the burglar. If she had run out it would have given the burglar a chance to escape, and she would not have enticed him into the other acts.

It's a good rule for survival to get out of an apartment or house the quickest way possible if you return home and find a burglar has been there. Remember: Inside your apartment or house you are trapped. There's no way for you to be sure the intruder has gone. Don't take a chance. Get out. Go to a neighbor's place, the manager of the apartment, or anywhere to get help. This single piece of advice could have saved Holly Monihan's life.

If, however, the intruder gets between you and the exits and there's no way for you to get out, then the situation becomes more dangerous. If it's a man-woman situation, and it usually is, the average woman doesn't stand a chance. The violence and brutality of such an attack is stunning. Very few women, even with long hours of training, could overcome such an adversary. The key word here is *escape*—not *subdue* or *capture*. Just get away. In a one-on-one situation, the element of surprise is of great importance. The intruder will expect a certain amount of fear and panic; in fact, he depends on it. Both of those elements, fear and panic, impair the thinking process and reduce an intended victim to a helpless state. Right now, after reading these words, go through your apartment or house and make a plan of escape. Rehearse it again and again until it is firmly imprinted on your mind. Imagine yourself being blocked in the bedroom, a man attacking. How to escape? Even if you cannot get out of the room, there are ways to protect yourself. You might roll under the bed and start screaming. For anyone to pull you out from under the bed will be difficult. You can kick and scratch from under the bed, while the attacker is limited in what sort of physical action he can take. Screaming is the one thing he doesn't want to hear, and there is no way he can shut you up.

The element of surprise, when combined with a degree of deceit, can be a reliable avenue of escape. If you are cornered and it is apparent the intruder is intent on committing bodily harm against you—i.e., rape—move toward him and surrender. The old "relax and enjoy it" idea. The move will probably surprise your attacker, and once you are close to him, even in his arms, there will come that instant when his interest in sex will overcome the chase. Remember, he stands between you and the exit: a sudden move around him or under his arms can set you free. If you have practiced the race to an outer door, you will win and the intruder will find himself alone in your apartment or house.

8

One of the problems in this field is that courses in self-defense, alarm systems, and other means of protecting oneself are time-consuming, expensive, and in many cases ineffective. The remedies suggested in *Survival* avoid those pitfalls. Here, for example, are other practical protective devices. Most bedrooms, even in small apartments, have an adjoining bathroom. For a small investment, a dead-bolt lock can be put on the inside of the bathroom door and a telephone extension installed in the bathroom. If Holly had equipped her bathroom with these two articles, once she discovered the break-in it would have been simple for her to have stepped into the bathroom, bolted the door, and called the police. The intruder would have been helpless. He would have had to batter the door down, which would have taken great effort and produced loud noise. He would probably have realized that his intended victim was calling for help. Under such threat the intruder would have left quickly.

In homes where the bedroom does not have an adjoining bath, a closet can be used for the same purpose. A dead-bolt lock on the inside of a closet door and a telephone extension in the closet provide a safe harbor for anyone under attack. Once inside the closet with the door bolted, a person is safe from further assault, at least until help arrives.

Another alternative is to install an alarm system. Commonly called "panic buttons," these inexpensive systems consist of a simple push button, usually hidden under a counter ledge or shelf. When the button is pushed, it activates a siren or gonging bell installed so that the noise will alert as many neighbors as possible. The bell or siren should be mounted high so it is out of reach of the intruder.

A reliable system can be installed for under two hundred dollars. I might also point out that if such a system is purchased, neighbors should be told about it and the sound should be demonstrated so that if it is used the neighbors will understand there is a serious problem and do something about it.

It makes sense to place panic buttons in several different locations. One alarm device is all you need. You may connect it to as many panic buttons as you feel are needed. For example, a panic button in the bathroom or closet, one concealed in the kitchen, and another in the sitting room would give good coverage in a small apartment. The cost per button is reasonable, about fifteen dollars.

There are some additional precautions that accompany such a system. First, the person or persons involved should practice running to the panic buttons at least once a week. When the time comes, and we hope it never does, that the panic button is needed, there must be no hesitation. When under pressure, a person must not be trying to figure out where the buttons are located. Believe me, if they are installed and then forgotten, that is exactly what will happen.

There is one last precaution, and it is important. I suggested the use of the panic button system in conjunction with a safe harbor—the bathroom or closet with a locked door between you and the intruder and a telephone at hand. That is the ideal use. If such a panic button is used when the intended victim has no safe harbor and is exposed to a reaction on the part of the intruder, there is real danger. Somewhere in that situation the victim must make a decision whether the risk created by using the panic button is less than the danger of allowing the intruder to carry out his intentions.

This is particularly true if the intruder is armed with a lethal weapon, a gun or knife or even a heavy club. The sudden sound of a screaming siren or clanging bell may trigger a deadly reaction. But remember, we are discussing the Holly Monihan case, in which, so far as we know, no weapon was involved. Situations where deadly weapons are involved will be covered later in the book.

Let's summarize the protective measures that are immediately available in the sort of situation Holly Monihan faced that night when she lost her life:

1. Escape is the key. When trouble or danger is apparent, get out of the apartment or house.
2. If escape is impossible, remember that fear and panic render you helpless. Avoid them by having a preplanned escape route or procedure. Preplanning consists of mapping out an escape route and practicing its use.
3. Avoid physical hand-to-hand combat.
4. Install dead-bolt locks on bathroom or closet doors and install telephone extensions in these "safe harbors."
5. Install panic buttons connected to a single alarm device.
6. Avoid the pitfall of carelessness. Do not provide opportunity for the intruder to select your residence. Remember, it only has to happen once and you're dead.

2

May 1980, 9:45 P.M. It was hot and sweltering under cloudy skies. Julio Lazaras moved back and forth between his car parked in the driveway and his home. His wife, Maria, stood on the front porch watching her husband load the Ford Mustang with clothes on hangers, a small suitcase, and several cardboard boxes filled with samples of his products. When he finished, he slammed the door and walked back toward the neat white one-story residence in Miami's northeast section.

Maria asked, "Did you lock the car, Julio?"

"No," he told his wife. "I'll be leaving in ten minutes; nothing will happen." He walked by her and entered the house.

Maria followed, scolding, "You shouldn't leave the car unlocked. All of your good clothes are there. It doesn't make sense, Julio. You wouldn't walk away and leave the house unlocked."

"Do it all the time, Maria. So do you, when you're working in the yard or over at the neighbors yakking about God knows what." He spun around, grabbed his wife around her waist, and pulled her close. "If it weren't for the kids I'd take you with me and we'd have a hell of a time in Tampa."

She pushed him back. "Don't start fooling around, Julio, or it will be midnight before you leave and that will mean an all-night drive. It's late enough now. Coffee is ready. I made it strong so it will keep you awake."

Julio grabbed at her again but she sidestepped around him. Maria was twenty-eight and very pretty, with the figure of a teenager; it was no wonder Julio had visions of making love before leaving. After all, he would be gone for a week and that is a long time for a thirty-year-old man to go without his woman.

Julio Lazaras was a salesman for the Miami Janitorial Supply House. Part of his territory was the Tampa area, and once a month he would load up his car and head north to service his customers. He always started out at night. Traffic was light and it was cooler, so he did not have to use the air conditioning, which saved a lot of gas.

It was 10:15 p.m. when Julio kissed Maria goodbye and got into his car. The clouds had parted, revealing a full moon. A slight breeze sliding across Biscayne Bay ruffled palm-tree fringes and brought some relief from the stifling heat.

Julio settled down for the long ride. Less than two miles along the freeway, Julio was startled by a man's voice coming from the rear seat. "Drive straight ahead to the next turnoff, down the ramp, then pull over and stop."

Julio felt the muzzle of a gun pushed against the nape of his neck. He remembered Maria's warning to lock the car. "I'll do as you say," he answered, "but you're wasting time. I don't have that much money."

There was no further conversation. The man kept the pressure of the gun muzzle against Julio's neck. Julio could just make out his figure in the rearview mirror. Ten minutes later, off the freeway on a narrow street traversing an industrial section of the city, Julio pulled up to the curb and stopped.

"Open the door and get out," the gunman ordered.

Julio still did not look back. He opened the door and stepped out onto the rough pavement. "All my clothes are in the car. Why don't you take what money I have and leave?"

The man did not answer. He pushed forward the seat and, keeping the gun aimed at Julio, climbed out. "Turn around," he commanded.

Julio heard the order. He turned slowly and saw the man for the first time. He was medium height, dark-skinned, a Latin type. His hair was bushy and curly, although Julio thought he was over forty years old. The gun in his hand was steady, and he did not seem unduly nervous.

Julio stared at him. "What are you going to do?" he asked quietly.

"I'm going to kill you." It was a simple statement of fact.

The hair on Julio's neck stood straight out. There was something about the man that supported his declaration. Julio remained calm. "Why? I don't know you. We are strangers; why do you want to kill me?"

"It is not what I want. It is what I must do." The man's voice was singsong and Julio realized he was strung out on something. The gunman continued, "It is too bad. I watched you say goodbye to your wife. She will miss you." Then, without any further warning, he fired.

The bullet caught Julio low in his belly, struck his spine, and turned up, cracking ribs and tearing lung tissue. He did not lose consciousness but folded up and fell to a sitting position with both hands holding his belly.

The stranger did not fire again. Without saying a word he stepped into Julio's car and drove away.

Larry Cormack turned off the freeway, headed down the ramp, then swung right onto the narrow paved street. His headlights picked up the figure of a man sitting in the street near the curb. He was rocking back and forth and holding his belly as though he were in pain.

Larry brought his small pickup to a stop and rolled down the window. "Got a problem, partner?" he drawled.

Julio looked up. "A big one. I'm dying. Some bastard shot me and stole my car."

Larry jumped out of the truck and gathered Julio in his arms. He placed him in the back of the truck and drove like a madman to St. Luke's Hospital.

Five hours later Julio left the operating room. Doctors told Maria he would live, but the rest of his life would be spent in a wheelchair. The bullet had severed his spine, paralyzing the lower half of his body.

Survival Techniques and Analysis

Julio Lazaras Case

Motives reflect intent, and if a victim is going to avoid serious conflict with a criminal that can lead to violence and killing, the victim must have some idea of why the criminal launched an attack in the first place. Usually it is clearly discernible and often the intent is announced by the assailant. In the Lazaras case murder was the motive. The assailant was intent upon murder from the moment he hid in Julio's car. From his words just before shooting he appeared to be under some sort of compulsion or orders to kill Julio. Maybe he was hallucinating under the influence of some drug. Julio seemed to think he was.

Before proceeding with a discussion of Julio's situation, there is one simple point I want to make. A number of people are murdered and raped or attacked in some manner by criminals who hide in the rear seats of automobiles and wait for a victim to appear. It is an ideal situation for the assailant. First of all, if he is watching a particular area

15

he can see an intended victim arrive and park his car. This gives him a chance to size the victim up and determine if the person meets the requirements for being victimized. For example, if the criminal's intent is rape, does the person who parked the car meet his needs? Does she turn him on? Or if the motive is robbery, does the type of car and the appearance of its driver give an impression of immediate cash, enough to make the attempt worthwhile?

Survival readers should put into immediate practice the following procedures when leaving their cars or when returning to them:

1. Never, at any time, park your car and walk away from it without being sure all of its doors are locked. Sounds like kindergarten advice, but there is no single piece of advice in *Survival* that is more important. *Lock your car*. Think about it, remember it, then do it.

2. When you return to your car, day or night, look into the back seat before entering it. Be sure no one is hiding there, crouched down and ready to attack after you get in the car. Make this a habit. There are hundreds of men and women who would be alive and well if someone had been able to convince them that such a precautionary measure was a necessity for survival.

If Julio Lazaras had read *Survival* before that fateful night and accepted its commonsense approach, he would be walking right now instead of being in a wheelchair. All he needed to know to prevent his tragedy was the two L's: Lock and Look. That phrase translated into time takes less than fifteen seconds, and can spell the difference between life and death.

After Julio had made his initial errors of failing to lock his car and failing to look before entering it, he was faced with a deadly dangerous situation. Nonetheless, there are several things he might have done in order to protect himself. It is a basic rule that when you are confronted with

16

an assailant armed with a deadly weapon, particularly a gun, you do as you are told. It is a good rule, but there are exceptions. That is why it is so important to understand what is motivating your assailant. How do you find that out? Ask. Many victims do it without thinking, their first impulse being to ask, "What do you want?" If Julio had asked that question he might have discovered the man was planning to kill him. With that knowledge he might disregard the gunman's orders, and, instead of slowing down and turning off the freeway, he could have speeded the car up. Now the gunman is in a precarious position. He himself is in danger and if he pulls the trigger there's going to be one hell of a smashup, which could easily kill him.

Let me repeat: If someone announces intentions of killing you and has the means, you might as well go all out. If you comply you're going to get killed, so you have nothing to lose.

That doesn't mean, however, that you should strike out in blind panic and fear. Remember, you are a thinking animal, and there are few unsolvable problems if you put your mind on them. Let's move right to the point where Julio was ordered out of his car and his assailant told him to turn around. It was at that point when Julio first asked the question "What are you going to do?" and the man answered, "I'm going to kill you." Now Julio was standing on a lonely and deserted street late at night face-to-face with a homicidal assailant. Could he have done anything to protect himself or was it too late for Julio to act?

The answer is: It's never too late. That, in itself, is a lesson for *Survival* readers. The end is not the end until it is the end. An average person who has not spent hundreds of hours shooting a handgun is probably very inaccurate with it. He can't hit the proverbial side of a barn. The instant his assailant announced his intentions of killing, Julio could have turned sideways, presenting a narrow profile to the gunman. Remember it was dark, or at least the lighting was very poor. Then Julio could have run for it: a dash for his life down the road or off onto the shoulder as a possible cover. I guarantee that if Julio Lazaras had taken such action he would not have been shot. To shoot a running man in poor light using a handgun takes a real expert, and even then the probability of hitting him is low.

I would particularly recommend running with a weaving or some other sort of evasive action. To do this, Julio would have had to remain in complete command of his senses. That is the advantage of reading *Survival*. The reader can formulate an escape plan even for the impossible sort of situation Julio Lazaras faced that night near Miami. The mere existence of an orderly escape plan is the key that will keep you from caving in to fear and panic. You should re-read the preceding paragraph until you are thoroughly familiar with its contents. A few minutes now may save your life later.

3

OFFICER PETE COLLINS SHOOK his head. "That hasn't been their pattern so far, John. Now don't get me wrong. I think they're extremely dangerous. Anytime stickup artists are using sawed-off shotguns, it tells me they're ready to do whatever is necessary to get away, and that includes killing." The officer, a veteran of 12 years, instinctively shifted his gun belt and holster so the butt of his .38 Magnum was touching his right hand.

John Wu-sang was no stranger to hazardous conditions. In 1977 he had placed his wife, Nancy, on his back and walked more than fifty miles to board a refugee boat at Kompong Som, Cambodia; as a result of malnutrition, Nancy was too weak to walk.

That was two years before John and his wife had worked their way to the United States and, with assistance from a refugee group, had purchased a small mom-and-pop grocery store in southeast Los Angeles. The business venture prospered and John Wu-sang felt happy and useful for the first time in years. Neighborhood people loved both him and Nancy. They provided food for families, and if money wasn't always immediately available, they remembered their own hard days and extended credit to tide less fortunate people over difficult times.

For three weeks there had been a series of small-business holdups in the surrounding area. Two black men using sawed-off twelve-gauge shotguns were terrorizing merchants.

Pete Collins had been riding a radio car patrol in the area for more than three years. He knew the merchants and liked them. They respected him and listened when he took the time to give them advice. Now Pete was worried. Experience told him that if the stickup men were not caught, they would kill someone. He didn't want it to be any of his people.

John Wu-sang was 56 years old, small, wiry, and dark-skinned. His wife, even smaller than he, was about four feet nine inches in height. She was younger by five years and in a soft quiet way was a very pretty woman. They both waited on customers in the store throughout long hours each day.

John smiled at his friend Pete Collins. There were gaps between stained teeth, the result of scurvy. "It's OK, Pete. No one will harm us. If they come here and need money so badly, I will give it to them." He shrugged. "They don't even need guns."

Pete growled. "You don't understand, John. These men are dangerous. If they come in, do exactly what they say. Don't make a move unless they tell you to."

"Mr. Pete," Nancy spoke up, "we are not afraid. John and I have faced death many times. He is not such a bad companion. You should learn to tolerate him." She bowed low in front of the big uniformed officer. "You know he will be your eternal partner. Everyone must accept him."

Pete Collins was six feet five inches tall. He weighed 250 pounds. His skin was so black his partners would say that at night you couldn't see him unless he smiled. Like John and Nancy Wu-sang, Pete had seen his share of trouble and because of that he translated his badge of authority into a means of helping people. People liked him and felt safe when he was on duty.

Pete now took off his hat and laid it on the counter, then wiped his forehead with a white linen handkerchief. "That's one way to look at it, Nancy. But I would like it better if these two bums stay away from my people." He put his hat back on and started out the door. "Remember," he said, turning around one last time, "you two don't move fast if these two show. Slow and easy is the name of the game if you want to stay alive."

Three hours later, at 5:15 p.m., there were three customers in the store. One was an 11-year-old boy who stood looking at the candy counter.

John Wu-sang walked over. "Yes, David, is there something I can do for you?"

David looked up and smiled. "I have ten cents. What candy can I buy so that I can share with my brother and sister?"

John rubbed his partly bald pate. "Now that is going to take some thought." He reached into the candy counter and removed five candy bars. "I have a special on today, David. You can buy these five bars for your dime. That will give you enough so that your dad and mom can each enjoy one."

David handed over the dime. "That's great, Mr. Wu-sang. Thank you for making it a bargain today."

Before John could answer, one of the other two customers shouted, "This is a stickup. Don't anyone move."

John Wu-sang looked up. Two black men stood in the center of his small store. Each of them held a short-barreled shotgun in his hand. "There is no need to shout or threaten us with your guns," John said calmly. "Come and take the money. It isn't much, but you are welcome to it."

Nancy was across the store from John. One robber was covering her with his gun. She started to walk toward John, who was still behind the counter.

The robber held his gun at waist level and moved closer to Nancy. "I said no one move!" he shouted, then pulled the

21

trigger. The shotgun blast caught Nancy in the belly, blowing a hole through her and killing her instantly.

John screamed, "No!" and jumped over the counter.

A blast from the second man's gun caught him in midair and nearly tore his head off. He fell across Nancy.

David ran out of the store screaming. He got away while the robbers were trying to shuffle new cartridges into their weapons. They ran out the rear door. No one else saw them.

Pete Collins stood looking at the bloody mess. It was five minutes after the shooting. He had been heading for the station to sign off duty when the call came of a 211-shooting at Wu-sang's grocery store, 190th Street.

Pete took his cap off and laid it on the counter. Again he wiped the sweat from his face. There were large drops around his eyes. Curious onlookers watched the big officer and turned away. They understood the difference between tears and sweat.

Collins shook his head. "Damn it, Nancy, I said no sudden moves." He paused, then added, "I hope brother death is half as good to both of you as you have been to all of us." Then Pete Collins put his cap back on and walked slowly from Wu-sang's grocery store.

| Survival Techniques and Analysis |

John and Nancy Wu-sang Case

We all visit banks, grocery stores, and other shopping centers every day. It's probable that at some time during

22

our lives, we will be caught in the sort of situation that occurred in Wu-sang's grocery store. It's important to realize that the survival wisdom that comes out of this case does not apply only to merchants or businessmen. If those robbers had been able to shuffle another shell into the chamber of their guns, David, the 11-year-old boy who was a customer, would also have been killed. As we examine the details of that tragedy, it is important to emphasize that not only could anyone in that store have been a victim, but he could have triggered the shooting even if John and Nancy Wu-sang had obeyed the gunmen's orders. If a customer had moved, the shooting would have started.

The first question that comes to mind in this case is why the gunman shot Nancy Wu-sang when it was obvious she was not trying to interrupt the holdup? To answer this question, everyone should have some understanding of the mental and emotional state of men who enter places with weapons and try to take what they want by force. Such men are frightened. They expect resistance and believe their chances of getting away with the caper are no better than fifty-fifty. They have hyped themselves up to the point where they are ready to die in their attempt to steal. They are also ready to kill anyone who tries to stop their robbery. In other words, they are dangerous, desperate men, and what would appear to be a perfectly innocent and normal move to anyone else could very easily seem to such men a dangerous and challenging act.

Very often such men are under the influence of alcohol or some other type of drug, and of course that makes their thinking processes even more unpredictable and dangerous.

The best advice to follow in such a situation is precisely what Officer Pete Collins offered the Wu-sangs: Do exactly as you are told. That is one of the important keys to survival when you are faced with a person who has a gun and is giving orders. Remember the other thing Officer Collins said: No sudden moves. Nancy Wu-sang wasn't listening and she violated both of those principles. The gunman ordered, "Don't anybody move." He expected everyone to obey that order, and if someone did not, that person would be defying him and his answer was to pull the trigger.

Now in the case of John Wu-sang, we must observe a difference. Once shooting begins, it is likely to continue until many people are down. Understand that until the first gunman pulled the trigger and killed Nancy Wu-sang, these two men were not involved in murder. The killing of Nancy changed everything in a split second. Now murder was involved and there were witnesses who could send the robbers away for life, even for execution.

Suppose you are involved in such a situation. When the shooting begins the first thing to do is hit the floor and remain there, motionless and silent. Once shooting starts, anything can happen. There is a psychology involved in shooting people or even animals. Somehow it is harder to point a gun and pull the trigger at someone lying prone and helpless on the floor than it is to fire at a running or moving target that can be considered a threat to the gunman's security.

I realize there are a lot of aggressive types running around who, if caught in such a situation, would feel bound to do something—to challenge or even attack the gunman. And furthermore, there are growing numbers of people these days who have mastered enough self-defense training to be capable of disarming a robber and subduing him until the police arrive. But in my view, there are many things wrong with that sort of approach in a situation like the one at Wu-sang's grocery store. First of all, there were two robbers involved—and I want to underline the fact that often, while only one robber is visible, a second gunman is

4

MILDRED JOHNSON WAS HAVING a difficult time with the final figures of a quarterly financial report which had to be ready for executive planning committee distribution at eight the following morning. Gerald Harding, vice-president and general manager of the small accounting firm, was looking over her shoulder. They were both tired. It was past nine o'clock on a cold, dreary, snowy night in New York City's middle Manhattan district.

"I still don't like it, Millie." Harding's voice was cold and impersonal. "The figures are correct but the presentation format is bad. There's a sense of chaos about it." He handed the 16-page report back.

Mildred accepted it and looked at her boss. At that moment she hated him. In his late thirties, slim, handsome, with just a touch of gray at the temples, Harding was a driver, a relentless, absolute perfectionist. "I'm worn out, Mr. Harding." She moved deliberately, placing the cover on her typewriter, then rising and walking over to the metal hall tree. She put on her tweed overcoat and wrapped a wool muffler around her throat. "I'm sorry about the report. It is the best I can do right now. There is no time to redo it, so unless you replace me it will have to do."

Gerald Harding was no fool. Women with Mildred's qualifications were hard to come by. "Don't be dull, Millie.

I understand. The report will be all right." He hesitated, then offered: "I'll come down with you and send you home in a cab. It worries me to have you walking at this time of night."

She shook her head. "No, Mr. Harding. My place is only a few blocks away, and I feel like walking. The snow and cold will help relax me." She opened the door, then turned back toward him. "I'll see you in the morning, and I really am sorry the report displeases you."

Before Harding could answer she had closed the door. He could hear her footsteps on the concrete floor as she walked to the elevator.

Outside, Mildred Johnson stood for a moment on Madison Avenue and let tiny snowflakes touch her face. She was 35 years old and had come to New York five years ago from Steubenville, Ohio. Short and too heavy to be attractive, she had never married and, with good insight into her personal problems, had decided long ago that a business career offered the best chance for some sort of success. She worked hard, and her dedication to the job together with a pleasing personality made up for what was lacking in her appearance. She was successful, able to maintain herself in moderate luxury on her $2500-a-month salary, and had a good feeling of belonging in the center of this monstrous city.

Madison Avenue was deserted even at this early hour. For a split second Mildred questioned the wisdom of walking three blocks to her apartment building. Then she shrugged and started north toward Central Park.

Mildred walked close to the buildings. They offered some protection from the veil of falling snow. She kept her head down and walked rapidly. Then it happened.

The girl from Steubenville bumped into a man. He stood directly in front of her. His voice was low and his words were mushy as they struggled to emerge from an alcohol-sodden brain. "Hey lady! You're kind of cute." He grabbed her by both shoulders and pulled.

Mildred pushed back but could not break the hold of those hands on her shoulders. "Stop it! You're hurting me," she cried out. Again she tried to twist away but couldn't make it.

The man was big and strong. "Come on, lady," he growled, pulling her into a recessed doorway, then pushing her into a corner. His body pressed against her.

"What is it you want?" Mildred demanded. "I have money. It's in my purse; just take it and leave me alone."

His right hand ripped the purse from her shoulder. "You're damned right I'll take the money, and then I'm going to have a little piece of your ass, lady. Right here I'm going to screw you. Bet you've never been laid on the pavement before." His hand dropped the purse and tore at the heavy tweed coat, ripping it open and laying bare one of her breasts.

Mildred fought like a tigress, with both hands clawing and scratching. Blood flowed from the man's right cheek as her nails dug a deep furrow.

The man fought back. His left hand caught her by the hair and bent her head back. As he leaned over to kiss her, she bit him on the lip and could taste the salty blood as it ran down her chin. Then the man exploded. His right hand smashed into her face, and she collapsed on the wet cement.

He leaned over her. "Want to play a little, lady?" He ripped her blouse off and tried to unfasten the hooks at the back of her skirt.

Mildred kicked and the heel of her right shoe caught his Adam's apple, pushing him back. She struggled to her feet and, for a moment, thought she would get away, but he grabbed an ankle and pulled her back down.

Then Mildred Johnson felt the knife blade. It plunged

into her side. He pulled it out and struck again. This time it penetrated her chest and for the first time she screamed. Loud piercing screams of terror.

Residents in the apartments overhead heard the screams and hunkered down, feeling safe in their own surroundings. Then they heard Mildred Johnson's last words: "My God, you're killing me."

Survival Techniques and Analysis

Mildred Johnson Case

During my career I've handled a good many cases in which the circumstances were almost the same as those in the Mildred Johnson case. And it always strikes me how unnecessary this shocking incident is. A tragedy so easily avoidable. The decision taken when Mildred Johnson stood outside her office building and questioned the wisdom of making that lonely walk was what ultimately led to her death.

I can't stress this enough: Avoid being alone at night in lonely areas. It's a piece of advice as old as the hills, and I suspect that no more attention is paid to it now than ever has been. The best and easiest solution to problems like Mildred's is not to put yourself in a position where such an attack can occur. Both Mildred and her boss considered the risks involved, and then they chose to ignore them. That was the first and crucial mistake.

Statistics, as dull as they are, become important in analyzing the causative factors which led to Mildred's death. In 99 percent of all such cases, the victim provided the opportunity for his or her own murder to take place. In the other 1 percent left, the victim had no choice, opportunity being provided by a stalled automobile or some other involuntary incident.

Although I hope that as a result of *Survival* a greater number of people will avoid potentially dangerous situations, I must assume from a practical viewpoint that men and women will continue to take unnecessary chances and expose themselves to the sort of attack that cost Mildred Johnson her life. For that reason I'd like to discuss all of the techniques which will provide some elements of survival after the attack is underway.

While it's true that a man or woman adept in the art of self-defense could have handled such a powerful head-on attack, for the majority of people this not an available option. The expense and the time element involved make it too impractical. The more realistic answer is, once again, *escape*.

Let's take a closer look at the Mildred Johnson case and discover why she seemed to have no chance at all once the attack started. One of her big mistakes, after she had made the decision to walk home alone, was how she chose to walk, that is, close to the buildings. Had she been walking next to the curb or, at that time of the night with little or no traffic, even in the street, her assailant would not have found it so easy to grab her and pull her into the recessed doorway.

Another mistake Mildred made was to walk with her head down. This might be more comfortable if it is snowing or raining, but it deprives you of warnings of danger ahead. If Mildred had been out on the curb or in the street and had been looking ahead rather than at the pavement, she would have seen the man who killed her, and at that point there would have been many options open to her. As it happened, her chances for escape were drastically reduced because she was not aware of the threat until the trap's jaws closed. The man had her by both shoulders almost at the same instant she realized he was there.

An intended victim can use several techniques given a few seconds before an attacker can actually lay his hands upon her. If the attack takes place on a city street, and most of them do, the chances are that along the curb there will be parked cars. When the intended victim, looking ahead, sees a person who seems to threaten, she can quickly step out into the street and walk toward the threatening figure, keeping the parked cars between her and the possible assailant. She needs only a few seconds' warning to accomplish this move. Even if she does not see the assailant until he makes a move toward her from a doorway or some other place of concealment, if she is walking on the curb line there will be sufficient time to jump out to the other side of a car and keep that car between her and the assailant.

Obviously, it will take some time for an attacker to catch up to his intended victim while trying to chase her around an automobile—and this gain in time can prove invaluable. There are other steps a victim can take. While keeping the automobile between herself and the attacker, she should begin screaming. For some strange reason women hesitate to scream. Probably it is an embarrassing thing for them to do, and they are afraid that they have misjudged the situation and will look foolish if their screams cause a commotion. That is a serious mistake. If nothing else sticks with the reader, this one admonition should: Scream. Scream loud. Scream for help. Better to make a mistake than to wind up beaten or knifed to death.

I am aware that there are all kinds of whistles and siren alarms on the market today. But such devices are no substitute for a good healthy scream. First of all, they do not impart the sense of urgency that is automatically transmitted by a scream for help. There are other problems with such a device. The victim has to locate it in her purse or around her neck on a chain or wherever she is carrying it. Then there is the effort required to activate the noise-maker while the victim is being chased or where there is struggling. The scream is a natural reaction to terror, and unless it is purposely stifled, little effort is required to produce a terror-stricken cry for help.

As for the listener, the person who hears the sound, clearly a terrified scream will galvanize a person into action much quicker than a whistle or siren.

I said the victim should place a car between herself and her assailant, and scream and continue screaming until help arrives. Another second step is just as practical. If the attacker appears to be gaining on his victim and about to catch up with her, she should remember that the automobile offers another way to prevent attack. If she hits the pavement and rolls under the vehicle the attacker will find himself at a distinct disadvantage. Before he can harm his victim he will have to drag her from under the car, and this will be no easy job. She can kick, and hang on to the underside of the vehicle. Remember, during all of this she can continue to scream. Facing such a situation, in 99 percent of the cases the attacker will take off. The entire situation has become too difficult and he will hunt for easier prey.

Eventually we must consider the point where the escape techniques have failed or have been ignored and the victim is in the grasp of her would-be assailant. Remember, I said the key word is *escape*, and even in this dangerous one-on-one situation, it still is. At some point in every such case the victim realizes she is fighting for her life, and I suppose terror and panic set in and she fights like a cornered animal. In most cases she will lose. First of all, terror and panic have robbed her of her best weapon, the ability to think. Now it becomes a contest of sheer strength, and believe me, the average woman is no match for an aroused man in that sort of a situation. Newspaper accounts and police reports are filled with that old cliché: "She put up a valiant fight for her life."

Many people wonder how a man can continue a sexual attack on a woman whom he must kill to subdue to his purpose. This introduces one of the key factors to escape in a situation in which the attack has come to bodily contact. One of the most important questions I considered while teaching at the University of Southern California dealt with just this topic: What is there about a rapist that drives him to the point of murder while he is engaged in an act of sexual intercourse? Every woman should know the answer to that question. For the true rapist, violence is a most important part of foreplay. Without a degree of violence he often becomes impotent. The greater the struggle, the more intense his sexual desires become. There are many cases on record where an intended victim has quickly agreed to become her assailant's partner without the necessity of violent struggle, and as a result the rapist has left without consummating the act. I must be careful to avoid serious misunderstanding. What I have said applies to the true rapist. There are many degrees of this sort of sexual aberration. Some men require only limited acts of violence, and often the attacker is not a rapist in the true sense but is only a man who feels the need for a woman. In this case it is probable that a violent struggle would deprive the man of his ability to consummate the sex act. These facts do not remove the immediate danger of death. Often after an act of rape the victim is murdered, not as a part of the sexual attack but rather as an afterthought, as part of the escape plan. The rapist figures that with the victim dead there will be no one to identify him.

Thus, regardless of what the motivating factors causing

the attack are, the victim is under threat of death. All of which reinforces the basic rule: Escape by trick and deceit is the best weapon.

Let's go back to the case of Mildred Johnson. You will remember that the man who killed her indicated two motives for the attack: first, he wanted her money, and second, he wanted to rape her. She offered him the money but decided to fight against the ravages of rape. Until she scratched his face and bit him on the lip he had not harmed her. It was a cold snowy night. If Mildred had carried her thinking about money to her body, the outcome could very well have been different. One has to wonder how a man already slowed down by alcohol would have performed sexually on a snow-covered sidewalk in near-zero temperature. If Mildred Johnson had not panicked she would have realized that at the point where her attacker had her cornered in the doorway she really had the advantage. First, she was sober. Her chances of deceiving the half-drunken man were excellent. Had she acquiesced to his demands and melted in his arms, there probably would have been several opportunities for her to twist away while he was concentrating on his sexual desires.

Now don't get me wrong. I'm not suggesting that Mildred—or any woman—should submit passively to the act of rape. I *am* saying that she should give the appearance of doing so. It is a matter of deceit. The intended victim gains time and places herself in a better situation as a result of her seemingly passive acceptance of her attacker's intentions. One of the greatest problems faced by a threatened victim is the fact that she has never considered the possibility of such a thing happening and therefore has no conceptualized plan of escape. Every woman who reads these words should study them until they are fully understood. Then she should plan her escape strategy.

In the majority of cases, escape is possible after the man

has been taken off guard by a pretense of acquiescence. But what if it isn't? Now the victim is faced with the fact of rape and the possibility of murder. What does she do?

There is one technique that is very effective and can be used as a last-ditch stand. It is almost a natural defense against the crime of rape. If the attacker is in full command of the situation and the victim realizes that escape is not possible, she should "faint." Now I'm aware that people are not able to faint at will, but what I'm suggesting is that the trapped rape victim should feign a complete and total loss of consciousness. Simply collapse. Become a sack of flour, a heap of meat and bone. It is a perfect defense against rape. Even if the rapist, after much struggling and tugging, can finally get his intended victim into position, if she remains absolutely passive with no sign of conscious life, he will find penetration next to impossible.

This tactic has another advantage. There is no struggle, and if the attacker is using force and violence as a part of foreplay, the sequence has been interrupted and his desires begin to diminish. With this totally passive approach the victim is not risking the chance of driving her attacker into a killing rage by hurting him. You remember Mildred Johnson fought and scratched and finally bit her attacker. Picture what might have happened if, while he had her backed into that doorway, she had suddenly collapsed into a pile of flesh and bones. Believe me, he would have had his hands full trying to do anything with her. The chances are he would have taken her purse and left.

Here, for the reader's convenience in reviewing, is a summary of the suggestions offered in this chapter:

1. Avoid giving an opportunity to a criminal. When there is a choice, don't place yourself in a position where an attack by a rapist-murderer would be possible.

2. For the average man or woman to become adept enough in the art of self-defense to be able to fend off a deadly attack is probably not a practical solution. Avoid one-on-one physical confrontation. Escape is the key.

3. When walking alone in a lonely area, particularly at night, stay away from buildings. Walk next to the curb.

4. Walk with your head up, alert to people, movement, and sound around you.

5. If a threatening figure appears on the scene, step out into the street and keep a parked automobile between you and a possible attacker.

6. If a chase begins around the car, remember to scream, scream, scream.

7. If the attacker appears to be catching up to you, hit the pavement and roll or scoot under a parked car. (In preparation for this sort of escape hatch, you should put on some old clothes and practice sliding under a car, so that you are confident it can be done.)

8. If escape techniques fail and bodily contact is made, remember that your ability to think is your best weapon. Do not panic. Do not fight: such violent activity will only intensify the rapist's desire. Use deceit, appear to surrender, and wait for an opportunity to twist away.

9. If all else fails, fake a total lapse into unconsciousness. A rapist will find it next to impossible to accomplish his act if he is struggling with a deadweight bundle of meat and bone.

10. But again, to avoid the situation where you might have to use steps 2 to 9 is the best answer of all.

5

JUNE 1978, SAN DIEGO, California. Jan and Henry
Stevenson were indoors reading their Sunday paper.
It was ten fifteen on a bright sunny morning and the
Stevensons felt relaxed and happy. Things had been going
well for Henry, and on Friday Jan had quit her job as
secretary to the president of a small manufacturing company. On Wednesday of that same week Henry had received
a substantial promotion and would now be considered as
top administrative officer in the banking chain he worked
for.

Jan was twenty-eight years old and Henry thirty-seven.
They had one little girl, age eight, and were anxious to have
another child. Wanda, their little girl, was playing outside,
enjoying the idea of summer vacation, which had just
begun.

Henry glanced at his watch. "It's ten twenty, Jan. You'd
better get Wanda in. She'll need to change for church."

Jan put down her section of the paper and stretched. "I'll
get her," she said, smiling at her husband. "You realize
tomorrow I don't go back to work? It's a good feeling to be
Mrs. Housewife again." She stood up and walked to the
entrance of their two-story home. Jan opened the door and
called, "Wanda. It's time to come in. Must get ready for
church."

For a moment there was no answer, then Angie Piedmont, the little girl who lived next door, came running up. "Wanda isn't here, Mrs. Stevenson. She's gone away."

Jan stifled a dreadful feeling. Little Angie must have meant something else. Probably Wanda had gone to the neighbors' house on the other side of the Stevenson place. "Did she go next door, Angie?" Jan asked in a calm voice.

Angie stood in front of Jan and shook her head. "No ma'am. She went away with a man."

Wanda's home was in the Point Loma district of San Diego, a high-income neighborhood whose homes reflected affluence and pride. They were mostly large two-storied places with four to six bedrooms. There were many children in the neighborhood who were constantly visiting playmates' homes.

Jan knew Angie Piedmont very well. She was Wanda's age and they went to school together. Angie had a habit of coloring the truth with a vivid imagination.

Jan stepped out onto the porch and stooped down, taking Angie by her shoulders. She spoke gently. "Angie. It is very important. What are you telling me about Wanda? You and I both know she wouldn't go off with a strange man. Where is she?"

Angie smiled. "Oh, I wouldn't worry about her, Mrs. Stevenson. The man wasn't exactly a stranger. He's been around a couple of days talking to us, and yesterday he asked me to go with him to the ice-cream place on Nimitz Drive, but I told him no."

Now Jan was thoroughly frightened. She called out, "Henry, come out here. Something has happened to Wanda."

Henry dropped his paper and rushed to the front porch. He recognized the fear in Jan's voice and knew she was not one to get upset over nothing. "What's happened, Jan?" he asked, then looked at Angie. "Where is Wanda, Angie?"

Angie told him the same story she had recited for Jan. When she finished, Henry stepped off the porch. "Jan, you go that way"—he pointed to the right—"and I'll go the other way. Keep calling. Go into every backyard. I don't believe Wanda would leave with a man after all the warning we've given her. She just wouldn't do it."

Angie was frightened now and she began to cry as she ran for her own home.

Twenty-five minutes later, at approximately 10:50 a.m., Jan and Henry met back at their home. They had thoroughly canvassed the neighborhood and there was no sign of Wanda.

Henry walked across the front room. "I'm going to call the police," he said. "They'll get the truth out of Angie. You know," he shook his finger at Jan, "that little girl has a great imagination. It isn't the first time she's come up with something that scared the wits out of us. Remember two years ago when she told us Wanda had fallen and broken her leg? We found out it was only a shin skin."

"I remember, Henry. But now I believe Angie is telling us the truth. Where else could Wanda be? We've checked everywhere she usually goes and no one has seen her."

Henry picked up the phone and dialed the operator. "Can I be of assistance?" the operator asked in a pleasant voice.

"Yes," Henry barked into the phone. "This is an emergency. Will you connect me with the police department."

"One moment, sir."

There was a slight pause, then a man's voice came on the wire. "San Diego Police Department. Sergeant Johnson."

"Sergeant, this is Mr. Henry Stevenson. My eight-year-old daughter has disappeared and her playmate tells me she left with a strange man in a car."

"Your address, Mr. Stevenson."

While Henry was giving the address, Sergeant Johnson was broadcasting it to the radio car in that district, and in minutes a black-and-white unit pulled up in front of the Stevensons' home.

The presence of the black-and-white unit made Jan feel better. At least something was being done.

Uniformed officers questioned Angie Piedmont for an hour before they came back to the Stevenson home.

Officer Harold Cummings explained the situation to Henry and Jan: "We believe the little girl next door is telling the truth. She's given us a good description of both the man and his car. Lots of detail, too much for her imagination. I've asked headquarters to send juvenile officers and investigators here. Our uniformed division will mount a search, so if Wanda is anywhere in the neighborhood we'll find her."

Jan and Henry remember the endless questioning and waiting. Hour after hour went by with no sign of their little girl.

The investigation continued for days. There never was any ransom note or contact of any kind from the man who had kidnapped Wanda.

Three weeks later, on July 9—Jan would never forget that date—the phone rang and it was a Lieutenant Stallman. "Mrs. Stevenson," he said, "is your husband home?"

Jan nodded her head as if the lieutenant could see her. "Yes, he's standing right here." She handed the phone to Henry and stayed close to him.

"Mr. Stevenson here. Do you have any news?"

Lieutenant Stallman's voice was soft. "Yes. Not very good. We found Wanda's body an hour ago in a ravine near the zoo. We have her in the morgue. I'll send a car if you're able to come and make a final identification."

Henry nodded. "Send the car. I'll be ready." He hung up and looked at Jan, then broke into tears. "They've found her, Jan. She's dead."

Jan Stevenson couldn't breathe. Her world had come to an end. She fainted.

Survival Techniques and Analysis

Wanda Stevenson Case

The Stevenson case exemplifies the cruelest of all crimes, kidnapping and killing a child. No one knows exactly what sort of torture the child suffers before death takes over. But we do have a feeling for the anguish, heartbreak, and loneliness of the parents.

This is a painful subject to write about, but it had to be a part of *Survival*. No book on how to protect yourself from criminal acts would be complete without an in-depth discussion of acts against children. It is essential for parents and children to know what they can do to shield themselves against the ever-present threat of kidnapping and murder.

There are three primary motivating factors, one of which is always present in any kidnapping case:

1. Kidnapping for money or other material gain. This is usually accompanied by ransom demands and directions.
2. Kidnapping as a tool of terror. In these cases a child or an adult is held as hostage until certain demands are met. Such demands are not for money but for political actions such as release of a prisoner or changing a political system.

3. Kidnapping of a child where the victim is a sex target of the kidnapper. Kidnapping motivated in this way can be directed against either a male or female child.

The last category is by far the most dangerous of the three. It is these victims who are most often murdered.

Generally speaking, the same rules and procedures will shield children against the three types of criminal. The basic crime in each case is kidnapping. If that can be prevented, then the secondary crimes—extortion, rape, murder—can be avoided.

A basic problem in shielding against kidnapping is a child's inability to distinguish a good person from someone who will harm him or her. A second problem presents itself when parents try to explain to children the necessity of avoiding contact with anyone who makes advances toward them. How is this accomplished without frightening the child to such an extent that his or her personality is influenced and he or she becomes afraid to exist in this world of ours?

There are no standard or pat solutions to these problems. Each child and every child–parent relationship is different. What would be effective in one case may fail in another. The best we can do in a book like *Survival* is to set forth some suggestions that are basically sound and hope they will be helpful in assisting all parents.

An error many parents make is failing to understand a child's capacity to remember warnings, dos and don'ts. Once a year, or even oftener, once a month or once a week, they might remind a child not to go away with a "stranger." That is not enough. Every day when a child leaves home or the immediate presence of its parents, a warning should be sounded. In order not to frighten the child, it should be couched in loving language and directed not from a context of fear, but rather from a context of loving care. As an

43

example: "You know how much mamma and daddy love you. If you go away with anyone without first coming to us and asking permission, we will worry and be very unhappy. So, before you go out, look at mommy and promise you won't go away with anyone without asking if it is all right."

In addition, the word *stranger* should not be used in warning a child. They are never sure what the word means. Who is a stranger? Is it someone they've never seen before? Was the man who kidnapped Wanda Stevenson a stranger? According to Angie, Wanda's playmate and the only witness, he was not. They had seen him for a couple of days and he had talked to them. It is probable that they thought of him as a friend and would exclude him from a warning against strangers. This brings up another important point. A large percentage of such kidnappings and killings are committed by family members and close friends of the families involved—who are definitely not strangers.

Parents can get around this by cautioning the child against leaving with anyone. If the reason for leaving is not to cause worry and unhappiness for mother and daddy, then it makes sense not to leave even with uncle or grandpa without first asking or telling mom or dad they are going.

There are several other methods to keep a child constantly alert to the dangers of kidnapping without frightening him or her. One novel idea that I am sure would be very effective is for parents to buy a bracelet and give it as a gift to their girl—or a man's identification bracelet to their boy. A few words engraved on the ornament would be a reminder: "We love you. Tell us first." When the bracelet is presented, parents might start a game. What the child "tells first" could be a secret between it and the parents.

Times have changed. In thousands of homes, mother and dad work. Even little children are more on their own than was true a generation ago. Children become responsible for their own safety at a much younger age, and therefore they must be made aware of all of the dangers which confront them in our modern world. It is not difficult for parents to warn against falling from high places, or running with a sharp stick in one's hand, or playing with a sharp knife. These are obvious dangers and children can understand them. But it is difficult for children to understand that there are people in the world who will sexually mistreat and kill them. The idea is grotesque even for an adult to comprehend.

Time is an important element in many such cases. Jan and Henry Stevenson spent precious minutes searching for Wanda before they notified police. Under ordinary circumstances this would have been acceptable, but Angie was an eyewitness and she told them Wanda had left in a car with a man. Angie had a description of both the man and the car. That information should have gone to the police at once. There should have been no waiting. If the little girl next door was using her imagination, no harm would have been done and the police would have soon discovered they were on a wild-goose chase.

However, in the event of ransom demands or in more complicated and delicate kidnapping cases, the question of when and if police should be notified becomes a difficult one to answer. I do not believe there is a universal answer. So much depends upon the state of training and experience of the individual police department and its officers. This is not meant to be an indictment of any law enforcement agency, but it stands to reason that unless agencies have received specific, in-depth training on procedures to follow when faced with the delicate problems often present in a kidnapping, their personnel can make serious mistakes which may result in death for a victim. It depends upon your degree of confidence in the local police agency. More and more, throughout the nation, police departments are upgrading their training. Requirements for recruits are being raised and many departments are sending officers to the FBI Academy in Washington, D.C. There are other fine academies scattered across the land. Large metropolitan departments establish and conduct their own academies and most of them accept for training officers from smaller departments that cannot afford to maintain their own training facility. I would suggest parents make it their business to inquire into the state of training of their local police agency. If it appears to be adequate, then there is no question about the wisdom of reporting a kidnapping immediately. The quicker the better. If a ransom note or any kind of warning about notifying police has been received, the person calling the police should be sure to tell them about it.

The kidnapping of adults by terrorists for ransom or political demands is more prevalent abroad than it is here, but the practice could easily spread. Executives of large companies, wealthy entertainment personalities, and anyone else who is in the category of targets usually selected by such terrorist groups or by individuals seeking large payoffs should have definite plans if they are hit. Those plans should be recorded and copies placed in the hands of attorneys and family members, and, if appropriate, registered with the local law enforcement agency.

The most important preplanning area is communications. When a kidnapping occurs, very often a victim is put directly in touch with attorneys or family members as a matter of proof that he is still alive. It is important that single words be assigned special double meanings so that a victim can covertly transmit information about his location, health, disposition of those holding him, etc. For example, the word "fine" could mean "I am being held by one person, there is no organization." The word "good" could mean "I am being held by an organized group." Those two words can easily be exchanged, and even if a message is spelled out by the kidnappers, to exchange them would be excusable.

If a person is in the category of those frequently kidnapped, he should make it a point to be sure at least one other person knows his plans for each day—where he will be and at what time. He should stay in close touch. There should be a regular check-in schedule, and if check-in calls are missed, the authorities should be notified and preparations made to handle a kidnapping situation.

Such a system is not nearly as restrictive as it sounds. Busy people follow tight schedules, and often every moment of their day is taken up. It should not be difficult for a busy executive's secretary, who has access to his appointments for the day, to make calls at proper times to be sure that her man has reached his appointment. This sort of an arrangement does not interfere in any way with the executive's time.

As for bodyguards, they are great so long as they are pros and know their business. They can protect against all sorts of attack, but I must be honest and tell you that if terrorists decide to kidnap you, they will undoubtedly know about your bodyguards. Before moving, they will know every move you make throughout a day. In such a case bodyguards are of little value. The terrorists will simply kill them and move in over their dead bodies.

If your position is one that obviously exposes you to a kidnapping scenario, there are other precautions that make sense. The use of an armored car in combination with bodyguards will provide what is probably the best all-around protection. I'm sure such protective measures are not practical for the average reader, but they are for the wealthy, powerful men or women who are targeted by terrorist groups.

Returning to the kidnapping of children, I should point out the great value of owning a dog. There's no question that a dog provides an immediate shield of protection for a child. Of course some breeds are better than others, but I have never been involved in a case or even read of one in which a kidnapper was successful when a child was being watched over by a faithful and protective dog. As a matter of fact, I had a personal experience with such a scenario. When one of my sons was about two years old, he was playing in the backyard of our home. The yard was fenced and an alley ran the entire length of our block. Mrs. McDonald was in the kitchen washing dishes in midmorning. She could see the whole backyard through a window. We had a large collie named Laddie who had been raised with our children and was very protective of them. Mrs. McDonald saw a man walking down the alley suddenly step over the fence and grab my son by his arm. That's as far as things went. Laddie charged and in seconds had severely bitten the man, who, bleeding from numerous slashing bites, staggered back over the fence and ran away.

Sometimes owning a dog is not practical, but when it is, there is no more effective protective screen available and the cost is within reach of most families.

One more idea is worth mentioning. Families should always have a photograph, no more than a year old, of each of their children. This is very important in case of kidnapping or in locating a missing person of any age. It isn't necessary to have a portrait, just a good clear snapshot which can be blown up to a larger size. When police are called into a case, usually one of their first requests will be for a recent photograph of a victim or missing person. Be sure to have one for them. Now for our summary:

1. There are three motivating factors in a kidnapping case:
   A. Money for ransom.
   B. Terrorism involving a play for freedom or power.
   C. Sexual gratification sought by the kidnapper from the victim.

2. Protective screens that are useful in any of the three categories will probably work in all of them.

3. Children should be warned against the threat of kidnapping in a way that will not frighten them unduly. A positive approach should be used.

4. Children do not have the ability to remember warnings over long periods of time; therefore they should be reminded every day to avoid contact with people they do not know, and that they should never leave an area with anyone—even a relative—without first asking permission of their parents or whoever is in charge of them.

5. The use of a loving reminder such as an inscribed bracelet is a good idea.

6. If parents have confidence in their police agency, they should notify that agency as quickly as possible that a child is missing.

7. A dog is one of our best defenses against the crime of child kidnapping.

8. Those threatened by a possibility of terrorist kidnapping should:
   A. Plan their day and be sure at least one other person knows that plan.
   B. Use bodyguards in conjunction with armored vehicles as a means of protection against attack.

6

IT WAS A LOVELY October evening.

Sarah Boardman walked close to the curb. It was hard for her to see anything because her eyes were overflowing with tears. It was her birthday and she was alone. Nineteen years ago she had been born in the home of her parents. It wasn't that they couldn't afford a hospital. Sydney Boardman was a successful Kansas farmer and had lots of money, but it was a tradition in his family that children should be born at home, surrounded by love. It was 1960 when Sarah first saw the light of day, and for 18½ years she had remained in that home. Three other children were born to the Boardmans. Sarah, the eldest, had decided six months ago that it was time for her to leave. Home, mother and dad, and her brothers and sisters were beginning to stifle her. She had tried working after high school but found it dull.

Sarah's parents understood what was happening to their eldest daughter but did not know how to handle the problem. They continued to insist that Sarah's place was at home, at least until she finished college, an idea which left the young lady cold. She had no intention of even starting college.

After weeks of discussion and argument they struck a bargain. Mother and dad gave Sarah a thousand dollars and air fare to Los Angeles. She was to remain on her own, make a try at getting along—job, friends, etc. A new life for Sarah. If things did not work out before she ran out of funds, she was to return home and spend the spring semester at college. That's as far as the plans went.

Arriving in Los Angeles in the middle of May, Sarah found a moderately cheap rooming house in the Hollywood area. She was able to find part-time jobs waiting on tables, clerking behind a counter in a large chain drugstore, and filling in as a ticket cashier for an all-night movie. She didn't like any of the jobs but managed to stretch her thousand dollars over four months.

It was during August that she ran out of funds and was forced to move in with another girl in the rooming house. Her roommate was Marion Cavanaugh, a twenty-eight-year-old prostitute, pretty and street-wise.

Since the time she left home, Sarah had contacted her parents only twice. Both times she assured them everything was fine and things were working out very well.

Two weeks after moving in with Marion, Sarah was flat broke. She had no prospects of a job, and all afternoon she had been alone in the small room trying to convince herself that she should call home, ask for money, and return to Kansas.

Sarah Boardman was a pretty brunette, just a trifle on the heavy side. Deep dimples on the sides of her mouth would sparkle and dodge in and out as she smiled and talked. Marion had been suggesting that the young lady from Kansas would do very well by taking dates with certain nice men who would be willing to pay well for her company.

It was still August when Sarah Boardman joined the ranks of street-walkers plying their trade on the sidewalks of the Hollywood area. She quickly discovered that the nice young men were "Johns," willing to pay for sex and many of them kinky in their demands.

Marion had been right. Sarah was pretty enough so that

her financial problems became nonexistent. She was able to maintain herself at slightly above the poverty level by turning a couple of tricks per night. She had put some money away and was planning on returning to her home just before Christmas.

Sarah had planned that homecoming a thousand times; in fact she was planning it as she walked home on this lonely birthday evening. She would bring nice gifts for everyone and still have money left in her bank account. No one in Kansas need know the details of her Hollywood adventure. She knew now that it would be fun to give college a try and meet a different class of people.

Someone honked a horn and Sarah was shaken out of her reverie. She dried her eyes and looked up. A blue van moved slowly along the curb. She recognized the man driving it. He was a John she had entertained on several other occasions. His first name was Harold; that's as much of a name as she needed in order to conduct her business.

Sarah looked at the tiny gold watch on her wrist. It was a graduation gift from her mother and father. The digital figures read 8:30 p.m.

"Hi, Sarah!" Harold shouted above the traffic sounds.

Sarah did not like Harold. He was a violent sex partner and on other occasions had hurt her with rough foreplay—spanking, beating, and choking. But he always paid well. Her usual fee of twenty-five dollars for a single trick didn't bother him, and he always gave a large tip, usually doubling the fee.

The girl from Kansas thought of her bank account. It was only a few months until Christmas. Then all of this would be over. She moved toward the van. "Hi, Harold. Feeling lonely tonight?"

The van stopped and its door swung open. "You said it, Sarah. I need loving. Hard as a rock. You'll get screwed to pieces tonight."

52

Sarah stepped into the van. "I can handle anything you've got, lover." She closed the door and the van moved away from the curb.

Harold's hand grabbed her thigh near the crotch. "We'll play in the van tonight. There's a nice bed in the back."

Sarah pushed his hand away. "I don't care where we play, but remember the rules. Cash in advance." She held her hand out.

Harold frowned. "You're a cold-blooded bitch," he muttered, reaching into his pocket. He handed her a roll of bills. "Take fifty, honey. I'll even give your tip in advance tonight, but you're going to get that little ass whipped."

Sarah counted out the money. She considered taking an extra ten but decided against it. Harold was cold stone sober and might notice the discrepancy. She handed the money roll back to him. "I took fifty. You can count it." She dropped her hand down between his legs and could feel the hard lump.

"I don't have to, baby." Harold put the money back into his pocket as he turned off on a side street and drove through winding roads up into the loneliness of Hollywood's hills.

Ten minutes later he parked. Both of them jumped out and walked to the rear of the van. Harold opened the doors and Sarah climbed in. He followed her and closed the doors.

Harold flipped a small switch near the doors and a dome light lit the interior. He was right. There was a king-sized mattress lying on the bed of the van.

Harold pulled off his shirt. "Strip down, honey. Here's where I get my fifty dollars' worth."

Sarah began to feel frightened. She had never been with Harold when he wasn't half out with the effect of too many martinis. They had never consummated their business in the van on other occasions. It had always been in her room or in a motel. She thought Harold was acting strange. There was something different about him. She made no move to disrobe. "I've been thinking, Harold. This is not for me. There's no toilet facilities. I can't clean myself up." She started to crawl toward the doors. "Let's go to a motel, or I'll give your money back and we'll call it off for tonight."

She was not prepared for his reaction. Harold reached out and grabbed her by the hair. He jerked her back, nearly breaking her neck. "Wait a minute, you little slut. I paid you and by God you're going to perform right now." He shoved her face down between his legs. "You've never given me a blow job, baby. How about it?"

Sarah jerked her head up. She was even more frightened. "Harold, stop it. You know I don't go that way."

Harold never answered; his hands wrapped around Sarah's throat and he began choking her.

Sarah tried to keep the panic out of her voice. "Stop choking me. I'll do whatever you want."

It was too late. Harold had slipped over the line of no return. His rage and desires were out of control. Always needing some violence to enjoy the sex act, now he was experiencing the ultimate. He was killing.

Sarah Boardman struggled. Her body thrashed about as Harold's strong hands cut off her supply of air. There had to come that instant when she knew he was not going to release his deadly grip and she was going to die. In that instant, Sarah Boardman had to think of Christmas, home, mom and dad, brothers and sisters.

There was just one thing. She thought of them too late. She was home for Christmas. On Christmas Eve her family gathered for a few moments at the grave in the public cemetery. In the silence of a cold starry winter night with a blanket of clean white snow covering the ground, they wondered: What went wrong? How did we fail?

Sarah could have answered their questions. They hadn't failed. She had.

Survival Techniques and Analysis

Sarah Boardman Case

When I was with the Los Angeles County Sheriff's Department, I spent two years in charge of the sex-crime desk at crime investigation headquarters. During that time I came into contact with many young girls like Sarah Boardman and learned a lot about what drove them to become prostitutes. Prostitution, particularly when it is practiced by young girls in their teens, is, at least in their minds, a necessity. It is a way for them to exist. Many of them have no work skills and are essentially unemployable. They adopt the prostitute role as a temporary measure. Like Sarah, they dislike what they are doing and they plan for a time when it will end. It will then become a closed chapter in their lives.

I am not condoning prostitution as an acceptable temporary condition. But under many circumstances it is excusable and understandable. *Survival* was not written for the purpose of examining moral standards and, with this in mind, I submit my second point. At the moment Sarah Boardman was being choked to death, she lost her identity as a prostitute and became a nineteen-year-old girl fighting for her life.

The Sarah Boardman case is not an illustration of the old clichés about never talking to strangers and staying out of cars unless you know who is inviting you in. Let's look more closely at Sarah's life. For at least two months she had been walking the streets plying her trade as a prostitute. She had certainly garnered enough knowledge to become street-wise. There had been times when she had encountered kinky sexual activities, and she knew that

Harold was strange in his sexual desires and that he required a certain amount of violence to enjoy the act. Yet even with this background, Sarah Boardman was not able to tell whether Harold was a man who could kill. She is not to be blamed for this, because no one can make these distinctions with enough certainty to be safe from attack.

I would like to discuss some facts that young girls and even older women should know.

To begin with, the sex drive in a man is the second most powerful instinct in his makeup, the first being self-preservation. As a man progresses through his own pattern of foreplay, he comes to a point where there is no turning back. The point of no return occurs for some early in foreplay, and for others it occurs just before ejaculation or climax. When a man reaches that point he is almost blind and deaf. He is acting under the influence of irresistible impulse and cannot halt the process.

What is the lesson of the Sarah Boardman case? It is this. Women must understand that the male animal can, when sufficiently aroused, commit murder. None of us are beyond it. One of the ways any man can be driven to the point where he will kill is through frustration of his sexual desires. Women must understand that to tease, excite, arouse the instinctively strong sexual desires, of a man without the intention of submitting to those desires, is a dangerous form of behavior. It becomes much more dangerous if there are indications of sexual kinkiness in the man's preferred form of foreplay.

Even a street-wise prostitute like Sarah could not accurately predict the behavior of a man when, after she had brought him to the point of no return, she tried to walk away. Although such circumstances have been used successfully as a defense in cases of rape and murder, I am convinced that Harold, when apprehended, should be tried and convicted of murder. Sarah Boardman's conduct on that night provides not the slightest excuse for murder.

I'm going to close the discussion on Boardman with a reminder to all women. Remember, man is the most dangerous animal of all when aroused sexually. Be aware of the potential for great bodily harm if you have aroused a man's expectations either intentionally or unintentionally and do not intend to submit to those expectations.

7

I T WAS APRIL 21 and the thermometer showed −20°
Fahrenheit, cold even for Minneapolis.

Harold Ellis worked hard at his job as traffic engineer for a threshing-machine company. They had hired him five years ago as a result of an interview conducted during his senior year at the University of Minnesota.

Harold had known he was being considered for promotion to chief engineer. Even so, it came as something of a shock when they called him into the corporate offices that afternoon and congratulated him. Donald Nelson, senior executive vice-president, shook his hand and said, "Keep up the good work, Harold. There's room at the top of this company for the right kind of men. We think you fit the bill."

Harold checked his watch: it showed 6:45 p.m., still early enough for him to stop on his way home and pick up a magnum of champagne so he and Lori, his wife of three years, could have their own private celebration. Harold Junior, 1½ years old, would be in bed.

When he left the liquor store, Harold drove slowly and cautiously. Snow was falling and visibility was poor. In his own block, where they had lived for two years, familiar sights were distorted by the curtain of snow, and he had an eerie feeling of being in a strange place. It persisted even after he turned into the driveway and waited for an automatic opener to lift the heavy double doors of his garage. When the doors were finally fully opened, lights inside the garage switched on automatically. Harold saw nothing unusual, so he drove in, switched off the ignition, and carrying the magnum of champagne under his arm, switched off the lights which activated the doors to begin closing. Then Harold stepped out of his garage and started toward his house a few yards away.

The light in the kitchen window cast a blurry glow toward the small backyard.

Harold hurried across the wet cement walk. He heard a rustling sound and then a voice called out: "Hold it right there, mister. Don't make another move."

The tone of voice was threatening. Harold could see the man. He was short and heavyset. Although it was hard to tell, Harold had the impression the man was young, in his late teens or early twenties. Harold stopped walking. "What do you want?" he demanded.

The man moved closer and Harold could see he had a revolver in his hand. He raised it up and pointed it at Harold's chest. "I want your money. That's all—nothing else. Just hand it over."

Harold suddenly realized the man was frightened. His voice was shaking and so was the hand that held his gun. "All right. Don't get nervous. You can have my money. There's over a hundred dollars. It's in my back pocket. Can I reach for it?"

The gun shook violently. "Go ahead, but move slow."

Harold had to do something with the magnum of champagne. It was under his right arm. He reached across and took it in his left hand.

The man in front of him stepped back. "Don't try to hit me with that bottle," he shouted, waving the gun. "Don't try anything funny or you'll get hurt."

59

Harold Ellis tried to keep fear out of his own voice. "I told you the money is yours." He reached into his right hip pocket and withdrew his wallet, then extended his hand with the wallet in it toward the thief.

The man reached out. Then, without warning, he pulled the trigger of the gun in his hand.

Harold felt the impact of hot lead tearing through his chest before hearing the explosive roar of the weapon. It felt as though someone had hit him in the chest with the flat side of a shovel. Then came the searing agonizing pain caused by the hot lead tearing lung tissue.

The bottle of champagne dropped from Harold's hand and he screamed, "Why? Why did you shoot me?"

The man did not answer; he turned and ran without taking time to pick up Harold's wallet.

Lori Ellis heard the shot. She knew it was about time for Harold to be arriving home. She was standing near the kitchen door when she heard Harold's screaming cry.

She tore open the back door and ran out into the yard. The man who had shot her husband brushed past her. She could only see a shadow; snow blinded her as she moved slowly forward. "Harold!" she called, "Harold! Where are you?" Then she saw him, a black lump on the white snow. He was curled up with knees close to his chin. "My God," Lori screamed. She knelt beside her husband.

Harold Ellis was dead. The bullet had severed his aorta and death was almost instantaneous.

The coroner's verdict was self-explanatory: "Death at the hands of a person or persons unknown at this time." What that report could not show was the shattered dreams of Harold and Lori Ellis, and a little boy's loneliness and disappointment at not being able to brag with the other kids about how great his father was.

Survival Techniques and Analysis

Harold Ellis Case

While it might appear at first glance that death was inevitable for Harold Ellis, I am firmly convinced that his death could have been avoided. He was challenged by a set of circumstances that he had never given any serious thought to or attempted to foresee. As a result, he found himself totally unprepared to handle the situation.

It is important for *Survival* readers to realize that the sort of thing that happened to Harold Ellis is not uncommon. It happens many times a year in this land of ours. The most difficult step in solving the problem is to get people away from the "it can't happen to me" syndrome. It is part of our mental protective screen to automatically deny that the terrible things that happen to other people could possibly occur to us. True, none of us can afford to go around every day worrying about whether all the tragic things we read about will happen to us. That is not necessary. But we must understand the perils which surround us and take sensible precautionary measures to prevent them from happening to us. Then, confident that we have done our best, we may go about our daily lives without fear.

Now let's take a look at how Harold Ellis might have prevented his tragedy. When he drove into his garage that night, he used an automatic door opener which turned on the garage lights at the same time it opened the door. It gave him a chance to look in the garage and determine that there was no one lurking there. Harold understood the

61

dangers of driving into a dark garage and prepared against the necessity of having to do that. He could have gone the one step further that might have saved his life. He had forgotten the area between his garage and his kitchen. There was no lighting in the area. For very little money Harold could have installed backyard floodlights operated from a switch in the garage or, even better, operated by the same switch which turned on the garage lights when the doors lifted. In the latter case, while still seated in his car, Harold could have seen not only the garage interior but the entire backyard area. If there was someone there, and there was, he would have seen him.

But Harold had not taken the precaution of backyard floodlights. He was faced by a gunman. What could he have done?

The reader must pay close attention to the following instructions. Place yourself in Harold Ellis's situation. A man is standing close to you, in the dark, with a gun pointed at your chest. He is demanding your money. The gun in his hand is shaking, and you sense he is frightened. What can you do? First of all, do not panic; do not add to the fear of the man with his wavering gun. Harold Ellis was killed by an accident. When his murderer was apprehended he said he had had no intention of shooting his victim. That was true. Frightened and panicky himself, he had seen threats in every move Harold had made. His pulling of the trigger had been almost an involuntary act.

Keep your eyes riveted on the gun and twist very slowly either to right or left, talking all the time to the gunman. You will find that to twist your body just a few inches, twisting at the hips and not moving your feet, will take you out of line with the barrel opening so that if the weapon discharges the bullet will miss you. Practice this movement with a friend and you will be surprised to find that in a few minutes you will be able to shift your body so smoothly and imperceptibly to a clear position that the move will not be noticeable to an overwrought assailant.

Remember to keep your eyes on the gun barrel. The man holding the gun will probably move it slightly. The trick is to keep your body out of line with the barrel opening so that if the gun discharges the bullet will miss you. While this is going on you should make every effort to comply with the gunman's orders. Give him what he wants as smoothly as you can. Explain every move to him before making it. Remember, he is frightened and panicky; it's up to you to calm him down. If you fail and he pulls the trigger, drop as though you were struck by the bullet, drop and lie perfectly still. Remember the assailant had no intention of killing you. He will probably be horrified by his act. He will not fire again but will probably run away.

I know the steps outlined here may seem complicated and difficult. Believe me, they are not. They are simple, easy to master, and highly effective. Before summarizing, I want to make one more point. If you are faced with Harold Ellis's situation and all else seems impossible or inadequate, there is a single move you can make which could save your life. Simply faint. Collapse, crumple down into a motionless heap. Do not move, do not speak. Have your assailant believe you have fainted or suffered a heart attack or seizure of some kind. The chances are all in your favor that the move will so disconcert your assailant that he will walk or run away. Now these points may be brought together in summary:

1. Prepare to avoid such situations by using automatic lighting systems, door openers, etc.
2. Imagine a man standing close to you and pointing a gun at your chest. Learn to use a twisting motion, twisting from the hip up and not moving the feet, to shift your upper body out of line with the hole in the gun barrel. Practice this maneuver with a friend until you have it down to perfection.

3. Remember the gun is what can kill you; keep your eyes riveted on it and counter every move by your own body shifting.
4. If the gun is discharged, drop as if you have been hit and lie motionless.
5. If all else fails, faint, collapse, fake a seizure, and your chances for survival will be excellent.

8

MARY SUSHINETTE GOT OFF the bus and walked rapidly toward her apartment in northwest Dallas, Texas. It was a pleasant spring day in mid April 1979. Late afternoon shadows were stretched to their four o'clock limit.

Mary's apartment was two blocks from where the bus let her off five days a week, Monday through Friday. She worked in a hospital as a practical nurse. Fifty-three years old and on the stout side, Mary lived alone; her husband had died three days before Christmas 1976. There were two daughters who lived with their families in other cities. So Mary joined ranks with thousands of middle-aged men and women forced to live alone and take care of themselves.

Harry Gordon lived in an apartment directly below Mary Sushinette's place. He liked Mary and made it a practice each day to be outside around 4:15 p.m. when she arrived home. Ten years her senior, Harry had ideas concerning his relationship with the widow but so far had kept them to himself.

He saw Mary turn the corner and called, "How's it going today, Mary? Were your patients able to stand you?"

Mary stopped and smiled. She liked the slender little man, and besides, there were times when she got tired of living alone. "I was good to them today," she told him.

"They'll be glad to see me in the morning. How did things go for you?"

"Same as always. Since I retired, I don't know why I get up in the morning. What are you doing for dinner tonight?"

"This is washday for me. I've got to hurry and get my clothes in those machines before someone beats me to them."

"But you've got to eat sometime," Harry pushed. "I'll pick you up at six; we'll go down to Bob's and have a steak."

Mary hesitated. "I'll be tired. Might not be good company tonight."

"You'll be fine. I won't keep you out late. Do we have a deal?"

Mary laughed. "We have a deal. I'll be ready at six." She hurried up to her apartment, and Harry walked to the corner where he bought a newspaper.

Mary worked fast. It was always a race to see who would get the washing machines first. She put her soiled clothes into a small cart, piled soap and liquid bleach on top of them, and headed for the elevator.

Three minutes later Mary Sushinette walked into a laundry room located in her apartment house basement. She began to put clothes into machines; her washing would take two of them.

She never knew when he entered, but Mary suddenly had an uncomfortable feeling someone was watching her. She looked up.

The boy was in his middle teens, blond and slender with a pimply face and tobacco-stained teeth. He was dressed in jeans and a loose sports shirt.

Mary was not frightened. She thought of him as a kid. "Why aren't you in school, son? Do you live here?"

The boy's voice was high-pitched. He was not smiling.

"School's out, lady. It's none of your business where I live."

"Now that's not a very nice answer." Mary straightened up and for the first time felt some concern. "If you don't live in this building, what are you doing here?"

The boy moved toward her. "I need money, lady." He held out his hand. "Give me what money you have and no one will get hurt."

Mary's maiden name was Murphy. She was Irish and had a temper to prove it. "Get out of here," she said sharply. She moved close to the boy and slapped him hard. "Get out of here. I should hold you and call the police, but you're not worth the effort."

He moved fast. His right hand, doubled into a fist, struck Mary high on the cheekbone. "Don't fuck around with me, lady," he hissed. He struck her again, this time in the stomach.

Mary had not met this kind of boy, who was unafraid and fierce, a product of our modern society. She had expected him to back away and apologize. Her cheek hurt and the stomach blow made her sick. "I don't have any money," she stammered, "just a couple of quarters for the machines."

He held out his hand. "OK, then we'll go upstairs and get what's in your apartment."

Mary handed him two quarters. "There are only a few dollars in the apartment, and my husband is there. He'll kill you!"

He stared at her. "OK. If we don't go upstairs, how about a little fucking? Ever been laid on a cement floor?"

Mary was frightened. She realized this "boy" was dangerous. "Don't touch me. There are people outside and right above us. I'll scream."

He made a quick motion with his right hand. As if by magic, a long-bladed stiletto appeared in his clenched fist.

"Make one sound, lady, and I'll cut your guts out." He slashed with the knife. It caught Mary on the side of her neck and blood flowed from a straight-line gash.

Mary knew her life was in danger. This boy was a maniac; he was going to have her or kill her and maybe both. She panicked and screamed, "Keep away," then launched an attack like a cornered animal.

Her assailant crouched low and began swinging the knife. Again and again his plunged its long, narrow blade into her body.

Mary Sushinette felt each cut and knew he was killing her. She stumbled and fell onto the concrete floor.

In seconds the boy was on top, plunging his knife into her chest and neck. He didn't talk, just growled like an animal.

Mary remembered him getting up and looking down at her. "Dizzy old bitch!" he shouted. He spat in her face, turned around, and walked out of the room.

Harry Gordon heard Mary's first scream and ran to an automatic garage door, which let him into a parking area. From there a door led into the laundry room. He had trouble getting his keys out. When the garage gate finally slid open and he rushed in, Harry remembered a blond teenager running past him.

He found Mary lying on the floor and knelt beside her. She was unconscious.

Before Mary Sushinette died that night at St. Luke's Hospital, she was able to tell the police what had happened and give them a description of the boy who had stabbed her.

Two days later Sergeant Fred Potter, working homicide, arrested Sydney Harris, a fifteen-year-old dropout who lived a block from where Mary was murdered. He lived with his parents, but like so many young people, Sydney did exactly what he pleased. He was totally out of control.

Within an hour of his arrest he admitted the Sushinette killing, and Sergeant Potter, a veteran of fifteen years' service, was shocked by his answer to the single question "Why?"

Sydney Harris looked at the sergeant and answered, "I wanted to kill her. She was a fat old bitch; no good to anyone. Better off dead!" He lit a cigarette and spat on the office floor. "What are you going to do about it?"

Survival Techniques and Analysis

Mary Sushinette Case

In case after case, we have seen evidence of the sickness that permeates America. There is an unbridled violence loose in our society, and no one is entirely free from its impact. Mary Sushinette is just one of the countless victims of random, senseless crime. What is particularly troublesome about her case is the commonness of the location.

Laundry rooms of large apartment complexes have become favorite spots for robbers and rapists. This is especially true when laundry rooms are part of underground facilities. They are isolated, and present an ideal situation for the prowling robber or mugger, who knows that many apartments are vacant in midday because both husband and wife work.

Some of the problem lies with owners or managers of large apartment complexes. Buildings are advertised as "security buildings," which leads tenants to believe they are safe inside. Nothing could be further from the truth. There is no such thing as a security building unless management hires reliable guards to be on the site 24 hours a day. Otherwise, the security measures most often used, such as keyed locks and automatic sliding doors, become traps and provide the robber or rapist with an operational haven made to order for his activity.

Tenants, therefore, should not rely on the security measures provided by many apartment house owners and managers.

Each individual must understand that to a certain degree security is a personal matter. In Mary Sushinette's case, I wonder if she was aware of the dangers of using the laundry room. Such awareness provides a foundation for commonsense security practices. If you are walking down a forest trail and the head ranger assures you there are no wild or dangerous animals near and you have nothing to fear, your built-in security triggers or alarm systems are going to be turned off. If the ranger has misled you and there is in fact danger, your chances of surviving have been considerably reduced because you are not alert or watching for danger signals.

In Mary Sushinette's case, there are several signals she might have noticed, if she had been alert. When she entered the laundry room she should have taken time to look around. There was a small half-bathroom, and that's where the murderer was hiding.

If she had looked into that bathroom, Mary would have seen him and walked out. At that point he probably would not have been in the mood for attack. Mary did not feel a need to look around. She felt safe, believing a security system would protect her; and, therefore, she neglected her own responsibility for personal safety.

When you use an isolated laundry room, make sure no strangers are present. Look around and check every spot where a person might be hiding.

There are other measures to be taken as well. The laundry room scenario is one exception I make to a general rule of advising women against carrying a weapon. There are several sprays available that incapacitate an assailant to a point where the woman can escape. Some of these sprays require permits, and in order to get such a license, instruction classes must be attended. Others, however, do not require a person to be licensed. There are sprays women use every day—hair sprays, dog-flea sprays, even washing-starch sprays. All of these, when aimed directly into the face, will temporarily blind an assailant and provide time for escape. A laundry room is an excellent spot to use such a method. Spray cans placed on a tabletop are instantly available and do not look out of place.

Mary made another bad mistake by refusing to walk back to her apartment. Remember, the kid suggested they go there to get more money for him. Had she agreed, they would have left the isolated laundry room, and Mary might have found an opportunity to escape. And, of course, there was always a chance they might have bumped into someone in a hallway or elevator.

Mary's final mistake was her attack. Until she slapped him, her attacker was not in a vicious mood. His first demand was for money. If she had satisfied that need, he might not have gone further.

This is an important concept *Survival* can impart to its readers. Young men and women today are capable of committing acts which a few years ago would have seemed impossible. Teenagers of both sexes will launch attacks intended to kill. Human life has become less important to segments of our society. The young boy or girl who accosts you and demands money or anything else is not the youngster of twenty years ago who can be frightened away by a display of force, but may be aggressive, vicious, and capable of committing murder. To understand this can save your life.

If Mary Sushinette had realized her danger at the beginning, she might have acted differently. The "boy" standing in front of her was not an ordinary immature youngster but a vicious killer, notwithstanding his age.

I have already discussed the value of installing panic buttons in private homes. The use of such a device in a laundry room, however, is a good idea only if the alarm is located where an assailant cannot hear it—in the manager's apartment or in building hallways where other tenants can hear and respond. When I previously discussed panic buttons I cautioned against their use if a victim was facing an armed assailant. The sound of an alarm might send him on a killing spree.

There is one further survival technique I have to suggest, and this is a dog. If a woman keeps a dog with her, there is no better protection. In reading thousands of case histories, I was surprised at how few times a woman or man had been attacked when accompanied by a dog. It almost never happens, and if it does, the assailant is usually driven off by the dog. I believe that if Mary Sushinette had been accompanied by a dog, she would be alive today.

It seems the size of the dog is not important. The mere presence of such an animal frightens the assailant off. I've talked to many men who have been imprisoned for all types of assault, including rape and murder. They universally say, "When there's a dog around, count me out!"

If the apartment house owner will not allow renters to have dogs, I believe a tenant has the right to insist on adequate protection—including panic buttons and security personnel on duty in laundry rooms. If management will not provide such security, then I am convinced they can be held legally responsible for damage if they refuse a tenant permission to own a dog.

9

M RS. GARCIA SHOOK HER head. "No, Mr. Williams," she said. "I do not want Larry to give up his opportunity for college. He's only eighteen. There's plenty of time for professional football."

Dick Williams smiled. "I'm not going to argue, Mrs. Garcia. If Larry wants a college education, he should take one of their offers." He turned to the tall, slender, dark-skinned Mexican boy who until now had remained silent. "Just one thing, Larry. In the four years you would devote to college it's possible to earn a million dollars above taxes. That would make Larry Garcia a millionaire. Then if you want to go to college," Williams shrugged, "have a go at it. Any university would be glad to have you."

Larry looked down at the bare wooden floor. The eldest of eight children, he had seen his mother and father struggle to provide a good home for them. His parents were born in east Los Angeles only a few blocks from their present home. Mr. Garcia worked for Los Angeles County in the mechanical department and had managed to support a large family without his wife going to work.

Two months earlier Larry had graduated from high school. For three years he starred as a fast, elusive tailback on the football team. All-conference and all-state honors were his, and offers from many universities poured in.

Three professional teams had contacted him since graduation. It was hard to make a decision.

Larry Garcia looked up. "Mr. Williams, I'm going to think about your offer until tomorrow. If you call at ten in the morning, I'll have an answer."

Dick Williams got to his feet. He was satisfied. Larry's interest indicated a good possibility of getting his signature on a contract. "Fair enough, Larry. Whatever you decide I know will be for the best."

Larry and his mother did not discuss the issue further but agreed to wait until Mr. Garcia came home. Then they would try to decide the best move.

It was a few minutes past four; Larry was watering a small patch of grass which struggled for life in front of the neatly painted green-and-white bungalow. Mr. Garcia had converted the garage into a bunkhouse where six children slept. Larry and his sister, Joan, each had a bedroom in the main house.

Larry watched the dry ground soak up life-giving water. All day he had been struggling with his problem. The professional offer meant instant relief from the privations his family faced. He felt a deep sense of loyalty and responsibility toward them. It should have been an easy decision, but for Larry it was not. Since he was a little boy he had dreamed of going to college and studying to become a lawyer. The dream had not diminished in intensity. Now it was possible for him to pursue that course, and he hated to give it up.

There was one thing for sure. Larry wanted to get out of the east Los Angeles area. Like all young men in the barrio, Larry was a member of his own neighborhood gang, the Alley Rats. They had dominated street and social activities for most of Larry's high-school years. Recently a new gang had shown up, the Street Trawlers. Competition between these two groups had been fierce. More than one killing had resulted from their activities during the current year, and Larry was frightened. He no longer wanted to play a part in their macho scenarios.

Friends had warned him that to drop out before he left the area would be dangerous. He was an important member of the Rats, and they would not take his defection lightly. An even greater peril existed because of Larry's prominence, which made him a prime target for the Street Trawlers.

Days were lengthening; in March sunset began at five o'clock and by six a hazy dusk enveloped the land. Larry had spent a long time watering the grass, but he had other problems. He could figure out answers better when alone. The sound of rushing water and the soft patter of drops hitting dry turf helped his concentration.

Larry frowned. Five days ago there had been an attempt by Alley Rats to crash a Street Trawlers party. Two Trawlers had been wounded by knife play, and word was out that the Rats could expect retaliation.

Larry had not been with those who had tried to crash the party, but as an Alley Rat he shared responsibility. His parents were unaware of the problem, but Larry Garcia knew something was going to happen. He could feel it in his bones.

"Larry, it's time to get washed for dinner," his mother called from the front door.

"OK, mom. I'll be there in a minute." Larry set the hose down and walked over to where he could turn the water off.

"Hey, Larry, how's it going?" The greeting came from a blue 1968 Chevrolet that had moved slowly up to the curb and now was parked directly in front of the Garcias' home.

Larry was leaning over the water faucet. He straightened up and turned around. "Everything's fine," he replied. He squinted at three young men in the car. Two were in front and one man was alone in the back seat. Larry thought he recognized them and started to walk toward the car.

"Talk is around you have a pro offer," the man in back called out.

About halfway to the car Larry stopped. He could see all three plainly and was startled to discover they were strangers. Larry wanted to run, but pride forced him to hold his ground. "Yes," he said evenly. "I guess you can say that. A recruiter was here today; we talked."

One of the men in front leaned out. "Are you going to take it, Larry? Are you going to leave us?"

Before Larry could answer, the man in back shouted, "I don't know if he's going pro or not, but I'm damned sure Garcia's going to leave us." With a single motion he raised a short-barreled shotgun, pointed it at Larry, and fired.

A full blast of twelve-gauge pellets struck Larry in the belly. He grabbed his stomach with both hands and tried to keep his bowels from tumbling out through an enormous gaping wound.

The blue Chevrolet roared away, and Larry heard a shout, "Fuck the Alley Rats."

Larry Garcia turned; he took five steps, then fell to his knees.

His mother heard the shotgun roar and came running out.

Larry held out his arms. "They've killed me, mama. I'm dying! God help me!"

Larry Garcia died only a few steps from where he had entered this world eighteen years earlier. Born into his mother's arms, he died cradled in those same arms. Dick Williams would have to look elsewhere to find a tailback who wanted to leave school and earn a million dollars.

Survival Techniques and Analysis

Larry Garcia Case

Almost every day a Garcia-type incident appears in the news. Gang-related crimes now seem nearly as common as fires and burglaries. My aim in *Survival* is not to lecture young people on the dangers of street-gang activities; and even if it were, I wouldn't be able to dissuade young men and women from joining a gang of their peers.

The only reason I include Garcia's killing in *Survival* is to emphasize certain points which are applicable to all of us. Larry Garcia was a bright, intelligent young man. He recognized the peril stemming from his membership in the Alley Rats. Friends warned him of danger, and he knew of the party raid that took place a few days before he was killed. He had a "gut feeling" something was going to happen. Even with all these warning signals, he decided to carry on as usual. It is this concept all of us should take heed of in the Garcia case. Violence and tragedy are usually accompanied by events which forecast their presence. If we learn to recognize signs of peril, then we have a chance to plan our protection. If, on the other hand, we choose to ignore the importance of those signs, we must be prepared to pay the price.

Now I am not suggesting that Larry Garcia should have been hiding away in his house or someplace else where there would have been no exposure to the type of gang activity he was expecting. Nothing that drastic. Remember, Larry was a member of the Alley Rats and had been for years. He understood gang dynamics—when, where, and how the Trawlers would probably strike. As he turned the water tap off and heard his killers' first greeting, things should have come together for him. Instead of walking toward them, he could have gone immediately into the house or run, making himself a difficult target.

I'm aware that some of those acts would have been against Larry's code. The gang imposes some strict behavior patterns on its members, and adherence to those patterns becomes a matter of pride. However, the rest of us don't have to follow any such code. When you or I or any thinking person recognizes events which threaten our lives, it shouldn't be hard for us to run from them. It's like when women feel too embarrassed to scream. When the chips are down and someone is trying to kill you, the Garcia lesson is simple: To hell with what others think! Do whatever you must to save your life, and that includes running, screaming, or any behavior which will be effective.

I mentioned in recounting the Garcia story that Larry had a gut feeling something was going to happen. This is a very important concept in *Survival*. Gut feelings are the same as hunches, premonitions, or a sixth sense. What are they really? How much attention should you pay to them? In order to understand their importance we must have some appreciation of how these phenomena occur.

The mind is the world's greatest memory system. It puts the modern-day computer to shame as far as memory capacity is concerned. Every sound, word, or visual concept you have seen, heard, or felt since you were born—and indeed even before, when you were still in your mother's womb—is accurately stored in your mind's memory bank. Failure in our human computer system is to be found in methods of recall. Material is all stored neatly away, but we have difficulty in recalling it from storage recesses. Sometimes, in fact very often, the mind itself recalls certain data without any assistance from us. If immediate surrounding circumstances parallel those which occurred in our lives or in the lives of others we have read about, memory recall can be triggered. We get the feeling of a hunch, a gut feeling, or a premonition. Our subconscious is trying to warn our conscious mind: These circumstances are dangerous; be careful!

All of this relates directly to the Garcia case. That afternoon when Larry Garcia knew something was going to happen, his subconscious memory was trying to warn him. In Larry's memory bank, recent events paralleled those of many occasions where people had been shot and killed as a result of gang activity.

His subconscious recognized these parallels, became alarmed, and tried to warn Larry's conscious mind so he would take steps to avoid being killed.

My bedrock advice, then, is for people to pay attention to their gut feelings, hunches, or premonitions. They are not products of black magic or superstition. They are products of a sophisticated protective system which exists in all of us. In those who have led a dangerously adventurous life, the system is much more pronounced because it has been constantly used. Usage sharpens the image. For those who spend their lives in a quieter manner, manifestations of the protective system are somewhat less well defined and more apt to be misunderstood. In either case we should learn to examine our hunches carefully in order to assign some value judgment to them. There are many people who are alive today because they paid attention to subconscious warnings.

10

JULIE HARRISON LIVED ON White Avenue near 7th Street in Grand Junction, Colorado. Her father and mother owned and ran a women's ready-to-wear shop on Main Street, just four blocks from the large two-story brick home they had purchased thirty years before when they first arrived in the small city of 25,000.

Julie had been born in the old Harrison place. She attended grammar and high school in Grand Junction, after which she went to Western State College in Gunnison, Colorado, where she majored in English. Upon earning her degree, she returned home and took a job as a reporter on the *Daily Sentinel*.

It was the middle of June 1979, and Julie went about her work feeling elated. In two weeks she would marry Bruce Hampton, a young man whose parents owned a peach orchard south of the city and who had been a schoolmate of Julie's since first grade.

After high school Bruce went to study agriculture at Colorado State University in Fort Collins. He had been raised on a farm and intended to stay in that business.

Julie and Bruce were sweethearts from the beginning. There had never been a doubt in their minds but that one day they would marry and raise a family in this lovely city on the western slopes of Colorado's Rocky Mountains.

The Hampton farm and orchard was six miles south of the city. A four-lane paved highway was available for five miles, then it was necessary to turn off on a two-lane dirt road which led to Bruce's home.

Julie finished typing a short item describing a church lawn fete. She pulled it from the typewriter and left it on the city editor's desk on her way out. It was past four and she was to meet Bruce at his home at four thirty.

Twenty minutes later, just a few yards from where she would turn off onto the dirt road, Julie's vintage Dodge coughed, sputtered, and died. She pulled off onto the shoulder and coasted to a stop at the intersection with the dirt road.

Julie was twenty-five years old, blond, slender, and pretty. She was wearing a light red-and-white dress, not because she wanted to, but because her boss was dead set against his female reporters running around in slacks. "Takes something away from them," he would growl each time the subject came up for review.

Julie got out of the car, leaned over and removed her shoes, and began to walk down the dirt road toward the Hampton farm. It was only a mile, and when she got there Bruce would send help to get her car started.

She had been walking five minutes when she heard a car approaching from behind her. She stepped off the narrow road and looked back. When the car, which carried three men in it, drew up opposite her, it stopped and the man in back opened the rear door. "Want a ride?" he called out.

Julie did not know any of the men, but she knew that the road dead-ended at Bruce's place and, on account of this, thought the men were going there. It was a bright sunny afternoon and she could see no reason not to accept the invitation. Besides, she was in a hurry.

Julie Harrison was a bright, modern, sophisticated young lady. She knew all of the reasons not to accept rides

82

from strangers. A year earlier she had covered a kidnapping and rape story of a young woman in the adjoining town of Delta, Colorado.

But the distance she had to go was less than a mile and nothing serious could happen between where she was standing and Bruce's home.

She stepped forward. "Thanks. I'm going to the Hamptons'," she said and got in. "My car broke down back on the highway. You must have seen it when you turned off."

"Yes." The man sitting next to her in the back seat spoke in a soft voice. "It was an old Dodge." He reached across her lap and slammed the door.

As the car pulled away, Julie knew she had made a mistake. The three men were young and clean-shaven, but there was something about them that frightened her. She thought fast. "I'm sorry but I left a package back in the car. I must have it."

The driver turned into a narrow side road which ran through Hampton's orchards. "We'll drive back. There's no hurry."

As the car came to a stop before completing its U-turn, Julie reached for the door latch. There wasn't any. It had been removed. Suddenly she remembered that when the man in back had opened that door, his arm reached out through the window and opened it from outside. Now the window was closed. She settled back and tried to keep fear out of her voice. "It's nice of you to take the trouble. Bruce Hampton and I are going to be married two weeks from today. Do you know the Hamptons?"

The passenger seated in front turned and rested his arm across the back of his seat. "No, honey. We weren't going to the Hamptons. Turned off on the road by mistake; thought it might take us to a spot where we could catch some shuteye. You see, we've been driving all night."

They picked up speed. The man seated next to Julie put his hand on her leg. She realized he was spaced-out. He rubbed her leg. "It's good you're getting married, honey. You see, the three of us are going to break you in. When we finish, you'll know everything a man can do for a woman."

Julie was terrified. The car swung onto the main highway without slowing down and headed south at a high rate of speed.

"My name is Conrad," said the man next to her. "What's yours, honey?" He pulled her close and his hand moved under her dress.

Julie pushed him away. "Stop it," she screamed. "I'm not the kind of girl you want." She begged the driver, "Stop this car and let me out. What kind of men are you?"

The man grabbed Julie's dress high on the shoulder and tore it away from her. "You're the kind of girl I want, lady. It's been a long time since old Conrad took a cherry." He leaned over her. "Am I going to get one, or have you been sleeping with that boyfriend of yours? You know, trying each other out?"

Rancher Homer Kyubeck testified at the coroner's inquest that he had heard a scream come from a wooded area about 5:30 p.m. He hadn't paid any attention to it because, he said, "Young people often use the place for parties and picnics and it is not unusual to hear screams coming out of there."

The coroner's verdict was murder and rape by unknown assailants. Julie Harrison had been gang-raped and choked to death. No suspects have been apprehended.

Survival Techniques and Analysis

Julie Harrison Case

The dangers of hitchhiking and accepting rides from strangers are so obvious that it amazes me that intelligent people ever do it. Right now, as I'm putting this book together, there are a series of murders in the Los Angeles area claiming young men as victims. It is becoming apparent that accepting rides from strangers is equally hazardous for men and women. A simple answer solves the problem: Don't hitchhike. Don't accept rides from strangers. But no matter how this basic piece of advice is presented, many people still choose to ignore it.

If asked why, most people point to the percentages. Of the tens of thousands of hitchhikers, only a small percentage are victimized—at least to the extreme of rape and murder. The possibility of such a thing happening is so remote that people ignore it. It's the "it could never happen to me" syndrome. The argument is especially tempting when circumstances become pressing. Julie Harrison had a date to keep and it was important to arrive on time.

The hitchhiker argues that it's like crossing a street. If you have to get to the other side, there's no choice even though dozens of people get killed every day crossing streets. You feel that if you're careful it will not be dangerous.

Unfortunately, there is no way of being careful when you are hitchhiking. How can you tell what a killer looks like? How does a woman recognize a rapist at first glance? Murderers and rapists have no outstanding physical characteristics. They look like everybody else.

While I don't agree that hitchhiking is an acceptable form of transportation, I am forced to acknowledge that it will probably always be with us. For that reason I will discuss those circumstances in which hitchhiking is even more dangerous than it usually is.

Obviously, hitchhiking is more hazardous at night. Also, if you must hitchhike, accept a ride only when there is one person in the car, unless it is a couple, a man and woman. Don't be in a hurry to get into a car. If someone stops and offers a ride, look the car and its occupants over carefully. Talk to them. Get a feel for the circumstances. Be sure doors have handles on the inside so you can't be locked in. Do not get in a back seat with another person. (If there's a couple in the car and they are both in front, it's all right to get in the back seat.) If a driver is alone in a car, always get in front.

Suppose now that you have gotten in a car with someone who is bent on doing you harm. Then what? Again, we have a one-on-one situation. Everything I've said before holds true here. *Escape* is the key. If you are in a car with only one other person and he is driving, you have an excellent chance of getting away. Remember, as long as the car is moving, the person behind the steering wheel is preoccupied with driving. Unless he is armed with a deadly weapon such as a gun, there is little he can do to harm you. Before beginning an attack a driver must stop the car, and at that instant there is an excellent chance for a hitchhiker to get away. Play a thinking game. Plan your escape, and be ready to move quickly.

If there is more than one person in the car, there are other precautions you can take. Remember I cautioned you not to get into a back seat with another person. If you are in the back seat alone, you have an opportunity to get out quickly when the car stops. Remember to remain seated behind the driver and to get out of the car on his side.

Otherwise, a passenger seated next to him can reach over the seat and keep you from getting out.

The chances are that when the assailant parks his car, it will be in some lonely spot where escape can prove very difficult. Nonetheless, an intended victim should try to get out and run away even under the worst of circumstances. Put off the final deadly confrontation as long as possible. If it becomes inevitable, if the final scenario is to be played out, what can a victim, either man or woman, do? In many cases surrendering has not provided an answer. Both young men and women have, after being sexually abused and tortured, been murdered. In most cases an answer cannot be found in this final confrontation. The victim has already lost. When a scenario has progressed to a point where it becomes the victim's physical prowess against the assailant's, or, even worse, against weapons, a victim is at a great disadvantage.

11

HELEN, COME AND STEADY this damned ladder or
I'll fall right into the tree and take everything
down with me." Patrick Connely balanced pre-
cariously on the top step of the ladder alongside a tall
Christmas tree. He had been working for hours decorating
and was ready to add the final touch, a huge silver star
designed for a tiptop position.

Helen walked in from the kitchen and looked up at her
husband. "Pat, you'll kill yourself and that will make a fine
Christmas for our grandchildren." She grabbed the ladder
and held it steady, but continued scolding. "You're no kid
anymore. Remember those dizzy spells you've had since
that inner ear infection. If one of those hits, you'll come
tumbling down."

Pat reached out and put the silver star on the very top
branch, then started cautiously down the ladder. "OK,
Helen, it's all done." He stepped off the ladder and gave his
wife a pat on her bottom. "You always worry. Fifty-five is
not that old, and by the way, don't forget you'll be fifty next
year."

Helen stood looking at the tree. "It's as pretty a one as
we've ever had, Pat." She turned to him. "Do you realize
this is the thirty-first tree you've decorated for us. Thirty-
one years. Time has gone fast, hasn't it?"

"It has, Helen. They've been good years. Just think, seven more and I'll be able to retire. With my city pension and Social Security, we'll get along fine."

Helen looked at a small gold watch on her wrist. "It's past ten p.m. You've got to get to work in the morning. A lot of people will be depending on your bus to get them downtown for Christmas shopping. There are only six days left. I tell you, 1979 has gone by so fast I can't believe December is nearly gone."

"Downtown looks very good this year," Pat mused. "Atlanta has always put on the dog for holiday seasons, but this year all our decorations are new. People appreciate it; they are shopping in the mid-city area much more than last year."

Before Helen could answer, a loud knock came on the front door. Pat and Helen lived in a quiet residential section of Atlanta. Southwest of midtown, it was an older section, but houses were well kept in a way typical of a middle to high-income area.

Pat frowned. "I wonder who that could be? Are you expecting anyone?"

Helen shook her head. "Heavens no, not at this hour. I hope there's nothing wrong with one of the children." They had raised three youngsters, two boys and a girl. All were married and in their own homes.

Pat walked to the door. "Who's there?" he called out.

There was a moment's silence, then a man's voice answered, "Parcel post. Package delivery."

That was good enough for Pat. He removed a heavy chain and opened the door.

Two men stood before him. They were Caucasians, in their thirties, both with long blond hair. Before Pat could say a word, they walked in and closed the door.

Pat knew at once he had made a mistake. He could tell from their clothes, dungarees and loose shirts, that they were not parcel post delivery men. "You said there was a package?" he demanded.

The taller one answered, "That was a damned lie, pop. We're not parcel post men." He took a small handgun from his pocket. "This should give you an idea of our business."

Helen cried out, "A gun! What do you want?"

The second man, several inches shorter than his partner, moved over to Helen and grabbed her arm. "Whatever we can get, lady." He was rough and shoved Helen against the wall. "Keep your mouth shut and maybe no one will get hurt."

Pat moved quickly. He pushed the man away from Helen and shouted, "Keep your hands off of her! Take what you want; there's no need to push us around."

The man spun around and drove his fist into Pat's belly. "I'll put my hands on her any time I want to. You shut up or I'll split your lip."

The blow doubled Pat up and he dropped to one knee.

Helen ran to him. She looked at the man who hit her husband. "Please leave us alone," she pleaded. "My God, mister, don't you know it's Christmastime? What's wrong with you?"

The man with the gun spoke. His voice was harsh and flat. "Go to the bedroom. I don't want to hear another goddamned sound from either of you."

Helen helped Pat to his feet and they walked slowly into a back bedroom. The Connely home had two bedrooms, one on each side of the house. They were separated by the kitchen and bath. It was an old home they had purchased twenty-five years before.

The man who struck Pat ordered them to lie down. He took short pieces of clothesline from his pocket. It took him a couple of minutes to tie Helen and Pat. He bound each one's ankles together, then rolled Helen and Pat over on their stomachs and tied their hands in back of them. Before leaving he warned, "Remember, not a sound. Just lie still and be damned glad you're still alive."

Five minutes later, Pat could hear them turning things upside down in other rooms. They were ransacking the place. He whispered to Helen, "I don't think they are going to harm us. If they were going to, they wouldn't have tied us up."

Helen was crying softly. "I'm frightened, Pat. Those men, there's something about them. I think they might kill us."

Before Pat could answer, the robbers walked in. The taller one spoke. "We haven't found a damn thing worth our trouble." He rolled Pat over onto his back. "Look, mister, you've got to have some money around here. Where is it?"

"There's about twenty-five dollars in my hip pocket." Pat tilted to one side so the man could remove his wallet.

The short man took a knife from his pocket and sat down beside Helen. "We didn't come here for nothing. If there's no more money we'll have to get our kicks some other way."

Pat grew more and more frightened. He felt now that these men were going to hurt them. "I'm sorry," he said as calmly as he could. "We don't have any more money in the house. I know it sounds dumb, but there's plenty in our bank. If you stay overnight I'll take you there. We can give you several thousand dollars."

"Now that's real nice of you," the gunman replied, "but there's not that kind of time. With no score here, we've got to make some other spot tonight. It's damned tough for you. Can't take a chance and have police notified, can we?" The gunman was standing over Pat. He didn't say another word. Pat watched him raise the nickel-plated revolver and place it an inch from his forehead.

Helen couldn't see what was going on, but she heard the ugly crack of a .32 caliber gun and knew they had killed her husband.

Helen Connely screamed. Terrified, she screamed again and again but there was no one to hear her.

The gun cracked again and Helen Connely died instantly, a bullet in her brain.

It was five minutes after eleven when Jack Nolan, Pat and Helen's neighbor, saw two blond men leave the Connely home. It puzzled him. He wondered what they were doing with Helen and Pat. Didn't seem to be the kind of people who fit Connely's friends.

Nolan walked inside and spoke to his wife, Elizabeth. "Liz, there's something funny going on at the Connelys'. I just saw two men leave there. Didn't look right."

Elizabeth frowned. "That's funny, I thought I heard someone scream a couple of minutes ago. Why don't you go over and see what's going on?"

Jack Nolan shook his head. "Not tonight, Liz. We'll wait until morning. If anything has happened that will be time enough to know."

It was cold and snowy that night in Atlanta. Neighbors, including Jack Nolan, will remember it as the night their good friends were murdered. Even now, a question remains who and why. Maybe one day there'll be some answers.

Survival Techniques and Analysis

Pat and Helen Connely Case

In this case we are faced again with the "it can't happen to me" syndrome. Given the conditions of society today, it is imperative for all people to understand that what happened to Pat and Helen Connely can happen to any of us. Tonight, tomorrow night, or a week from now, we may be sitting in our homes when that knock is heard. Each of us, as we walk to the door, should think of Pat and Helen's story. There have been occasions when robbers and murderers have crashed their way through a door or intruders have broken in when people were asleep in their homes. Those are different circumstances and we'll talk about them later. But in Pat and Helen Connely's case, the murderers were almost invited in. If someone is going to kill us, let's not help. We should make it as tough as possible.

I totally disagree with the line of argument that says this advice isn't always practical to follow. It is not difficult to ascertain who is standing outside your door. I'll grant it takes a little time and some care, but I guarantee you if Pat Connely had it to do over again, he would take all of the necessary steps to be damned sure who he was letting into his home. There's no way around it. Opening the door to a stranger is dangerous.

The simplest way to ascertain the identity of a person standing at your front door is to install a good wide-angle peephole in the door and to make sure there is enough light outside so that you can see anyone who is there. Peepholes are inexpensive and easy to install: there is no excuse for not having one.

One potential problem, even with wide-angle peepholes, is that often a person is standing out of the peephole's viewing range. There is an easy solution. If you live in a house and the surface outside is adaptable, paint a neat colored spot large enough for anyone to see. Place it where someone standing on it will be in full view when you look through the peephole. With such an arrangement, you can ask anyone to stand on the colored spot. Problems develop with this system if you live in an apartment house where there are carpets in hallways or other restrictions that would prohibit painting a spot. In that case, use a doormat. One with a backing which will adhere to the carpet is best. Be sure it is placed so that a person standing on it will be in full view through the peephole.

So now you have a peephole and you are able to see the person on the other side of your door. Let's consider the situation in which a person knocks and says he is delivering a message, but you don't recognize him. How do you handle that?

Remember, Pat Connely knew the second those men entered his home they were not delivery men. He sensed this because of their appearance, clothes, etc. He would have applied those same standards if he viewed them through a peephole. Every company in the business of making deliveries should provide their personnel with proper means of identification. You can examine such identification adequately through a peephole. Don't be timid about asking for proper identification. If a person does not have it, do not let him in. Even when you are expecting a delivery, these procedures should be followed. Hoodlums, murderers, and robbers will keep watch outside, and when a delivery van stops in front of an apartment house they will follow the legitimate delivery man in. Then they will go to another apartment and assure the occupants of their identity by asking them to look out the window where they can see the delivery van. Do not consider admitting delivery personnel, maintenance personnel, or anyone without proper identification. There is nothing embarrassing about asking strangers for identification before letting them into your home.

There is one other procedure which will help an ordinary person protect his home against tragic circumstances, and it's a good one. Outside doors should have mail slots in them. It doesn't make any difference where a mailbox is. A slot will permit delivery of messages, telegrams, etc., through a door without the necessity of opening it. Even if a signature is required, the delivery person can shove papers through a slot and they can be signed and returned.

Before we consider what we should do if, through carelessness, we admit a robber, rapist, or murderer to our home, I'd like to discuss the issue of keeping guns. I've been very cautious about advising people to have weapons in their homes. If there are children in a home, the presence of weaponry presents a deadly hazard; but that hazard is inversely proportional to the degree of care with which weapons are handled. *Survival* is written for the benefit of thinking, responsible people. It has not been thrown together for the purpose of making a few bucks. Therefore, its contents must, in a serious and thought-provoking manner, examine all avenues of safe conduct which will afford reasonable protection against attack.

I, for one, do believe that people should arm themselves in their homes. It seems to me that living in modern America, or any other place in the world at this time in history, demands that if a man is going to protect his family and possessions he must have the means to meet and repel the onslaught of those who would steal from and murder him and his family.

Let me immediately make a few qualifications. Only if a man or woman has taken the time and effort to become acquainted with and proficient in the use of guns would I recommend that they be kept in a home. To be properly qualified in the use of handguns takes time, money, and serious effort. Unless you are so qualified, I would recommend against considering guns as a means of protection in your home.

There are, however, other weapons you might consider if you are not qualified to handle a gun. A spray can could very well provide sufficient interruption of an assailant's attack to allow escape. In the Connelys' case, a handgun was involved almost immediately after the criminals entered their home. Pat and Helen were under threat of instant death from the beginning. If, however, Pat and Helen owned weapons and were well-versed in their use, the entire scenario might have been played out differently. (See Epilogue.) But as it was, the Connelys were helpless. They had made no plans for such an occurrence. That such a thing could happen was beyond their comprehension. Once intruders had entered their home, they had to believe in their own minds that the only chance was to do as they were told.

I speak of weapons in the plural because more than one should be available to the occupants of a house. Weapons should be distributed around the house in strategic places so that, when they are needed, they can be easily retrieved. Weapons can include spray cans, kitchen knives, a baseball bat, an electrically operated cattle probe which can give a shock heavy enough to stun a man, and a heavy book which can, when swung forcefully, knock an assailant unconscious. (The same book, by the way, is an excellent protection against a bullet. The average cheap handgun of low caliber will not penetrate the cover and pages of a large dictionary or atlas.) Also, the heavy bottles usually found in a kitchen make excellent weapons, even better when filled.

These are weapons which, for the most part, are commonly available around the home. Even so, some thought and practice are required before they can be used effectively. Identify the weapons in your home. Discuss and demonstrate their use with your spouse. Develop plans so that if your home is invaded everyone knows what to do.

We're talking about saving your own life. It's better to go down fighting than to be slaughtered like sheep. A well-planned counterattack can succeed against heavy odds because of the element of surprise. An invader does not expect resistance. It can make him panic and earn enough time for escape.

There are several basic rules for such planning. It is good practice, when under attack from intruders, to separate. In Pat and Helen's case, if they had planned resistance to such an attack, when Helen first saw a gun and realized she and Pat were under siege, instead of running toward Pat she might have run into a bedroom. Such a move would have forced the intruders to separate. If there had been weaponry available, Helen might have had a chance to use it. Such action would have split the attention of the assailants and could have provided some chance for escape.

In an earlier chapter I recommended that people under attack in their homes should run out as quickly as possible, but this applies when the intruder or intruders are unarmed, and the victim is not faced with the possibility of instant death. Also, in the Connelys' case, no opportunity of leaving the house presented itself. The techniques given in *Survival* must be chosen to fit the individual case.

Here are some other basic rules. People should have a method of communicating with each other in the presence of assailants without those assailants knowing or understanding. Simple hand, eye, foot, or head signals can be developed by using natural movements such as scratching one's head, blinking eyes, removing glasses, and licking lips. There are dozens of possibilities. Each such code movement must forewarn the partner of a specific action. For example, I scratch my head with my right hand; by prearrangement you will understand such a move means in ten seconds I will break and run for the bedroom. Or I'm going to go for one of our strategically placed weapons and strike with it. There are two important things about a code system. First, the partner must signal back that the message has been received and understood. When I scratch my head with my right hand, you lick your lips to tell me you have received, understood, and agree with my course of action. If you fail to acknowledge my original signal, I will conclude you either don't understand it or you do not agree and are advising against my move. A second important element is the specific time increment. Each action designated by a signal must have a specific time allotted for its beginning. Every time increment starts from the first signal. This gives a partner an opportunity to prepare for action and be ready to move in coordination with the planned escape or attack.

We've talked about panic buttons before; they could have saved the Connelys' lives, if hooked up to an alarm system which would be inaudible to intruders but would alert neighbors that an extreme emergency existed and to notify police at once. Make a deal with your neighbors today to install such a system. Costs are low. Arrange to have panic buttons terminate in the house or apartment on either side of you and let the neighbors do the same, with a terminus in your home or apartment.

To summarize the suggestions which would be most helpful in the event of a Connely-type attack:

1. Don't get caught in the "it can't happen to me" syndrome. Remember Pat and Helen Connely were good solid citizens like you, fine people. It happened to them and it can happen to you.
2. Never open your door until you know who is standing on the other side. To do so is an act of carelessness which can cost you your life.
3. Have a good wide-angle peephole installed in all outside doors.
4. Have an arrangement, either a painted spot or welcome mat that you can ask someone on the outside to stand on, so that you can get a good view of all visitors.

5. If the person asking admission is a stranger and appears to have a legitimate reason for asking you to open the door, demand good identification. If he or she does not have it, don't, repeat, don't let the person in.
6. Outside doors should have mail slots in them. This provides a way for small parcels or letters to be passed without the necessity of opening a door.
7. If you are properly qualified (check qualifications with an arms expert), have at least one gun in a convenient place where you can get at it in an emergency.
8. Keep other weapons available and know where they are: spray cans, heavy books, kitchen knives, baseball bats, a cattle probe, etc.
9. Develop a plan. Talk about it. Practice it. Prepare for an emergency by knowing what each person will do if it occurs.
10. If under direct attack, do not remain together. Split up if possible, to make the intruder or intruders split their attention.
11. Develop a method of communicating with each other so that an assailant will not know you are doing it. Make a game of this communicating system and become proficient in its use.
12. Have panic buttons installed in your home with responding alarms placed in neighbors' homes and allow them to place alarm system termini in your home.
13. Locks on bedroom, bathroom, and closet doors can create "safe harbors" and a telephone extension in these safe harbors can provide a lifeline. (*This is one of the most practical suggestions.*) If the Connelys had provided such a safe harbor in their home and had practiced getting to it, at least one of them could have reached it. Their assailants would have hesitated to shoot the other one because a witness would be left who could identify them.
14. Finally, remember you are a thinking animal. No situation is completely impossible. Fight to maintain emotional control. If you have planned carefully, chances for survival are good.

12

THE PARK IS BEAUTIFUL this time of the year, isn't it?" murmured Paul Miller. It was early evening of a cool September day in Estes Park, high in Colorado's eastern range of the Continental Divide. Paul sat on a canvas camper stool in front of a small tent and watched his wife, Mildred, finish the supper dishes.

"Remember when we were here for our honeymoon two years ago? It's been a special place for us," Mildren said as she set an iron frying pan down and walked over to her husband. Her hand ruffled his hair. "Maybe next year there will be three of us."

"Maybe; at least we can keep trying." Paul poked at the ground with a crooked stick. "I've been thinking about that offer from the Holly Sugar Company. I'm what they need—a good accountant. It could be a great opportunity."

"It's all right with me, dear," Mildred said as she sat down beside him. "Will it mean moving from Montrose?"

"Probably. For the first few years they'll want me at their main office in Denver. You know they have an office in Montrose, and at some later date I could request a transfer. Do you mind making the move?"

"Not at all. Denver isn't far from Montrose. Mother and dad could drive over any time. I think it would be rather fun." Mildred pulled her stool over closer to her husband.

They remained silent, watching the flames of their camp-fire flicker and leap about like something alive.

"The old man's mad. The old man's mad. Watch out, he's liable to hurt us."

The raucous remarks came from a campsite adjoining Paul's. He looked up and saw three men in their early twenties standing around a fire. Paul was surprised. Earlier in the day at this campsite, he and Mildred had met the Abbots, an elderly couple from Oklahoma City. Both in their late sixties, they had confided that this was their first camping trip and the idea of sleeping in a tent with sleeping bags was making them a little nervous.

"We're not bothering you. Why don't you go about your own business and leave us alone?"

Paul recognized Tom Abbot's voice. He got to his feet. "Tom may need a little help. Let's take a walk over there; maybe if we show up it will cool things down."

"No, Paul," Mildred objected. "Let's not get involved. It's only an argument. Let Tom take care of it himself."

"What's the matter, old man? Can't you and your wife make it anymore? How would she like a piece of this?"

Paul was watching and saw one of the men unzip his trousers and expose himself. That did it. He spoke sharply to Mildred. "Stay here. I'm going over and give Tom help." He walked rapidly toward the Abbots' campsite.

"Button your trousers." Mildred could hear Tom Abbot's voice. "You're all three drunk. Now get out of here." She saw him walk toward the three men.

Paul had not yet arrived at the Abbots' camp. Mildred could see him walking through a small clump of trees.

One of the men grabbed Tom and held him while another hit the older man hard in the stomach.

"Leave him alone!" It was Tom's wife: she was screaming.

Mildred jumped to her feet and ran toward the Abbots' camp.

"Let him go," Mildred heard Paul order. She knew her husband was afraid of what might happen. Paul had a violent temper. He was a big man, strong, young, and not afraid to go in swinging.

"Well, we've got a busybody," one of the three men taunted. "If there's anything I hate, it's someone who can't mind their own business."

Mildred stepped out of the clump of trees in time to see the man who'd been expressing his views on busybodies move toward Paul. He stood close to her husband. "That means you, mister. Get the hell out of here or I'll break your goddamned face."

Mildred moved over to where Mrs. Abbot was standing. They were now close to Paul.

Tom Abbot was still being held with his arms pinned.

The man confronting Paul was over six feet and heavyset. He looked tough. His eyes were bloodshot and he wasn't so drunk that he couldn't move fast. He was obviously ready and willing to fight.

Paul sensed danger. The third man of the trio remained quiet and in the background, but he was watching. There was no doubt Paul and Tom were outmatched.

"Well, what about it, shithead?" The man pushed Paul with the palm of his left hand. "Maybe the chick with you would like a piece of me?"

Paul swung hard. His clenched fist landed under the ear of his assailant. Paul swung again, this time with a solid left to the belly.

The man holding Tom let go and moved in fast. He hit Paul flush on the nose and blood spouted. Paul dropped to one knee. His nose was broken and he felt sick.

Tom Abbot rushed in to help, and the man who had originally challenged Paul kicked out hard, catching Tom in his groin. Abbot dropped, writhing in pain.

Paul was back on his feet when he heard the third man order, "Back up and let me have a shot at him."

Mildred was paralyzed with fear. Tom's wife had run to her husband's side and was kneeling over him. It seemed to Mildred Miller that everything was happening in slow motion. Both men who were attacking Paul backed away from him and the third man moved closer. Then she saw the gun in his hand. It looked big and he seemed to be carrying it casually.

"Paul!" she cried out. "He's got a gun."

Paul heard and swung around to face the number three man. "OK, mister, you win. Let's call it quits; I can't argue with a gun."

The other men joined their friend. Now all three stood close together. "Shoot the son of a bitch, Nick. Belly-shoot him," Paul's original attacker muttered.

The man with the gun talked slowly. His voice was high-pitched. "If I hit him, we take off right now. No fucking around?"

The other two agreed.

Paul was desperately looking for a break. "Hey! What are you talking about? Shoot me over an argument? Let's walk away from it, then nobody will be doing time for murder."

"I'll make a deal," the gunman said. "Let each of us have a bang at the women and we'll walk away. No one hurt. Everybody happy."

Mildred screamed, "Paul! Let it happen! It won't harm us and nothing is worth your life. Paul, listen to me. I love you."

"Your lady has the idea, mister." The gunman smiled. "She's right—we won't hurt them. They might even enjoy a little variety."

Paul Miller moved fast. He charged straight into the gun. He moved with the speed of a snake but not fast enough.

The gun, a .45 Colt automatic, roared. A heavy lead slug caught Paul high in the chest and slammed him back to the ground. It was as if a mule had kicked him.

After the gun discharged, all three men broke and ran.

Evening quiet returned and all Mildred could hear was the crackle of branches as they were consumed by the Abbots' campfire. She ran to Paul and knelt beside him. His face was turned up toward the sky, both eyes open and staring. Mildred knew he was dead.

Survival Techniques and Analysis

Paul Miller Case

I have deliberately included two cases in *Survival* that occurred in park areas. This is to drive home the point to my readers that danger and peril do not disappear from their lives simply because they are on vacation and away from urban areas.

A killing like Paul Miller's is particularly disturbing to me. The Abbots and the Millers were on vacation, enjoying themselves and not interfering with anyone else's right to do the same thing. I'm always struck by the fact that ordinary people, good people, you and I and all of our friends, can be caught in such a situation, which is much more common than anyone likes to admit. Campsites, even in state and national parks, are sometimes very isolated. Park rangers are not able to cover vast areas assigned to them on a regular patrol basis. So, when trouble begins, very often campers are on their own. The way we handle ourselves under pressure becomes all-important. It can mean the difference between living and dying.

When Paul Miller died that night in Estes Park, he had nothing to do with the circumstances which brought about his involvement in a situation that cost him his life. The beginning of that chain of events was beyond his control. However, from the instant he decided to become involved, his own decisions brought him face to face with the lead slug that cut him down.

I most emphatically do not mean to suggest that people shouldn't get involved in trying to help neighbors, friends, or even strangers when it is obvious they are in trouble and need help. In fact, I would advise exactly the opposite. Offer help wherever and whenever you feel it is needed. However, you must not overcommit yourself. For example, say you come upon someone who needs an emergency heart operation. Unless you are properly qualified, you should not attempt to perform it. That would be overcommitting yourself and you wouldn't be doing any good for the person in trouble. The lesson of Paul Miller's death is found in understanding the importance of knowing your own limitations. Know what you can do with the tools available and remain aware of the dangers posed by overcommitment.

Let's take another look at the circumstances of that evening. Paul heard rough talk and realized that his new friend Tom Abbot was facing trouble. He could see three men threatening to harm Tom and his wife. He made a decision to help and moved in. It seems obvious to me that anytime one man pits himself against three young men where circumstances indicate physical combat is possible, he is overcommitting himself unless he has qualifications which prepare him to handle such overwhelming odds.

There were, however, ways in which Paul could have aided Tom that would have been safer and more helpful. If he had been aware of the dangers of overcommitment, Paul Miller might have left his own campsite and gone away from the scene of trouble to get help in the form of rangers or other men or whatever. There was no immediate threat of serious physical harm when he initially became aware of trouble. The first thing he had to do was admit to himself that he could not handle the situation alone if it got out of hand. That's a hard thing for a man to do, but it's the lesson of that tragic night in Estes Park.

Paul Miller did eventually realize he was overcommitted, and he arrived at that realization before the gun appeared. When Paul was knocked to his knees and knew his nose was broken and he was going to take a severe beating from those three men, he should have broken and run for help. There was a certain sense of bravado and bullheadedness in the action he took. Paul had ceased to be a thinking animal and was striking out blindly. I cannot repeat too often the admonition to *keep thinking*. In a class I taught for the United States Army during World War II entitled "Kill or Be Killed," at least two hours each day were devoted to developing the ability to continue thinking under any and all circumstances. If you are shot, don't give up, keep thinking. If a bayonet runs you through, don't panic, keep thinking. No matter what happens, keep thinking and you have a chance for survival. Panic, freeze, or act under the pressure of pure fear, and whatever chance you might have had will be gone.

That has to be even more important when you have responsibility for others' safety. Paul Miller, by his final actions, exposed his own wife, Mildred, and the friends he had come to help to even greater danger. It's lucky the intruders didn't murder all of them. As it was, they ran off and left three witnesses, all of whom could identify them. This, I believe, is further evidence that Paul Miller was to some extent responsible for the situation getting out of hand. Readers should understand that what appears to be, at first glance, a minor argument or disturbance can suddenly erupt into a serious and deadly confrontation. Paul moved too quickly. He failed to consider what could happen if the circumstances at the Abbot campsite took a turn for the worse. He should have listened to Mildred at that point. What was happening was within his view. There was plenty of time for him to size up the situation and make a rational decision.

Even up to the final moments, there was an opportunity for Paul Miller to avert tragedy by remaining rational. The gunman offered to make a deal: the harassment would end if Paul would allow all of them to rape the two women. Paul's smashing attack, diving straight into the muzzle of that .45 automatic, was a clear indication of his giving way to sheer panic. Remember, Mildred shouted at him to "let it happen." I'm not suggesting Paul should have let his wife and Mrs. Abbot be raped, but he demonstrated, once again, his inability to think under severe pressure. If he had accepted the deal, all sorts of precautions would have been required and every step would take time. In such a situation time alone is an important ally. At any given moment, other campers could become curious about what was happening. Hikers or campers might stumble accidentally onto the scene. Also, it was entirely possible that those three drunk men might have left themselves wide open during their preparations for carrying out an attack on the women.

Paul Miller gave up all of those opportunities when he launched his suicide attack. There were other things Paul forgot to consider, as well. Besides himself, there were three other intelligent people present and on his side. Time could have given any one of them an opportunity to assist or break up the attack. Paul's action deprived them of any such chance. When you are faced with a situation as serious as the one Paul faced that night, play for time. Do not force the issue. Give everyone involved a chance to contribute. Remember, a dead hero is soon buried and forgotten. His glory ceases with his life and as a corpse he is of no value to those he loves.

I have some final suggestions that apply to the situations of all people who are vacationing in our national or state parks. Immediately after establishing your campsite, it is a good idea to become familiar with the shortest route to help. Where is the nearest ranger station or telephone? You should also know the approximate times when park patrols are due in your area. If Paul Miller had known a patrol was due to arrive in 15 minutes or even an hour, he could have played for that amount of time. These precautions are not only effective against attack by human enemies; they are equally useful in the event of snakebite or animal attack. A sudden illness or accident often requires help, so knowledge of where and when that help is available is important.

13

MARION LUDWIG WAS IN a hurry. It was past four on a rainy afternoon and her three children would be home from school waiting for their afternoon snack. Tom, Marion's husband, got home around six and would want his dinner right away so that it would not conflict with the Monday night basketball game on television.

Hard rains were not unusual in Oakland, California, during March. But when Marion drove downtown this day to complete her weekly shopping, the rain and wind made driving difficult. Marion usually left her car in a supermarket parking lot, but today she decided to use a city parking structure next door to her shopping area where she could stay under a roof and not get soaking wet. She had to drive up to the third floor before finding an open slot; this annoyed her because she would have to push her shopping cart up steep ramps when she returned. There wasn't room in the small elevators to accommodate her large steel wire pushcart.

It took more than two hours to complete her shopping and the wheeled cart was crammed full. Marion, in her early forties and a bit on the heavy side, had to stop and rest several times before reaching her car.

She pushed her cart to the car's trunk and was busy transferring brown shopping bags into it when she heard a man's deep threatening voice: "OK, lady, give me that purse."

Marion spun around. Facing her was a man neatly dressed in slacks and a pullover sweater. He was clean-shaven, tall, slenderly built, and she guessed him to be about thirty years old. He was black.

Marion's purse was slung over her shoulder with a heavy leather strap. There was more than two hundred dollars in it, which she could not affort to lose. For the first time, Marion Ludwig realized what a lonely and isolated place the third floor of a parking structure could be. She looked around and there was no one in sight. Her voice trembled when she spoke. "No! You can't have my purse. Now go away and leave me alone."

The man looked around, then he turned away as if to leave.

Marion felt a wave of nausea sweep over her. She had been badly frightened and sat down on the rear bumper.

She heard footsteps and looked up: the man had returned. He had a metal bar in his hand. Marion later described it as a "jack handle." Without saying a word, he struck her in the face with it. The bar's end caught her in the left eye, and as Marion Ludwig fell she chould feel her eyeball dissolve and run down her blood-drenched cheek.

The man remained deliberate and calm. He reached down and removed Marion's purse, opened it, and took what money was in it. Then he placed it in the car's trunk and knelt down beside his victim.

He spread Marion out on the concrete floor and raped her.

Marion did not scream, nor did her assailant speak a word or utter any sound. The scene was like a silent movie. Marion later told police that she was in a half-conscious state and the rape had seemed unreal to her.

Two weeks later, this same man attacked another woman, again in a parking structure. This time he caved in her skull with the steel bar and she died. Marion had just left the hospital where doctors had tried, without success, to save her eye. They were able to mend a crushed cheekbone, but she would carry an ugly scar for the rest of her life. When she read a newspaper article reporting the murder, Marion remembered her own ordeal and felt lucky to be alive.

Survival Techniques and Analysis

Marion Ludwig Case

Downtown urban parking structures, like subway tunnels, provide an ideal environment for crime. They are isolated and difficult to police without assigning permanent patrol personnel—and that is too expensive an item for most budgets to handle.

When a crime like the Marion Ludwig case occurs, there is often a cry for more police protection. It is a natural reaction, but, because of the economics, it does not solve the problem. There have to be other ways to prevent these increasingly common attacks.

I've heard a lot of criticism regarding one practice that some law enforcement agencies have begun to utilize in this area of crime. They keep a running tally of such crimes, asking local newspapers to print the information. There are advantages and disadvantages in this method of keeping people advised of dangers that exist within their city. One disadvantage people point to is that to publicize these incidents plants the idea in other minds, and as a result there is an increase in such crimes. Those in favor

111

insist that the opposite is true. Printing details of these crimes alerts the public and warns criminal elements that they cannot hope to get away with such acts.

I am in favor of publicizing the crimes. If there is a serious threat to the safety of citizens in any given situation, I believe they have a basic right to know such a danger exists. It is only with this knowledge that an intelligent person can take necessary precautions to avoid such dangers. It seems to me that it is the responsibility of local newspapers to carry such warnings.

Once people understand the dangers inherent in areas such as parking structures, they can begin to take whatever steps are necessary to reduce hazards. For example, during daylight shopping hours women should be constantly alert to the presence of other lone individuals, especially men. It is a good practice, when you drive into a parking structure and park, to sit in the car for a moment or two and look around to be sure there are either enough people walking about to ensure safety or, if there is no one and you are alone, to be certain there is no individual lurking or standing about. If for any reason you feel insecure, don't take a chance. Start the engine and leave. Remember, as long as you are in your car and it is locked no one is going to have an opportunity to harm you. The car is a safe haven. Not only are you protected from an immediate attack, but you have wheels under you and can leave at will.

If you are in a situation such as Marion Ludwig found herself in, where it is necessary to spend time loading your car trunk, you should leave the front door standing open so that you have a place to go in a hurry if something happens. Do not become completely absorbed in loading the car so that you are not aware of the approach of a stranger. If you see someone approaching, get into the car and close and lock the door.

112

If it's nighttime and you know the parking structure is unattended by guards or parking personnel on the premises, you should avoid the area altogether. This goes for both men and women. Such structures, usually located in downtown areas or at airport facilities, become dangerous traps after dark. In city-owned structures where there is no charge for parking, it is understandable that economics prevent the hiring of guards; but where a charge is made there is no excuse not to provide good security. One of the things a well-informed citizenry can accomplish is to insist that free parking be eliminated and a sufficient amount charged to provide for security.

Lots of attacks have also taken place in ordinary street parking areas. The same rules set down for enclosed parking structures are applicable, although open parking areas are less dangerous because they are not enclosed. They don't afford a criminal as much of an opportunity to carry on his activities out of view. But many business establishments have had to provide attendants and guards for their customers even in open parking areas, particularly after dark. There may be a legal responsibility to provide security for patrons when there is evidence that an area is attracting hoodlum types.

Now suppose all else fails and a victim finds herself in the position faced by Marion Ludwig when her assailant approached her and demanded money. What should a woman or even a man do?

The first rule is to give up your money. Additional crimes often occur when a criminal meets resistance to his demands. In the case of Marion Ludwig, if she had immediately given her purse to the man who blinded her, there was a good possibility that he would have left without harming her. Statistics show that once violence begins, it tends to lead to more violence, rape, or even murder. The most likely reason for this is that violence changes a criminal's mental attitude. Until violence occurs, he is not in so deeply that it is impossible to walk away. But once an act of violence takes place, his commitment is far greater, and if a victim is hurt it's not so easy to walk away. The injury binds an assailant to his crime by physical evidence.

There are other things Marion could have done that might have saved her from injury. If she had given her assailant the purse he would be busy, at least for a moment, in taking money from it. Marion could have run to the other side of her car and started screaming. With the car between her and the man, she would have forced the man to begin a chase, and, as I have already pointed out, to chase a victim around a car is not the easiest thing in the world. Remember when we discussed the mugging and murder of a woman on New York's Madison Avenue and pointed out that a woman could roll under a car and get a great deal of protection. Marion Ludwig could have used that technique. I guarantee if she had, the man who blinded and raped her would have run from the scene—provided Marion kept up a good healthy screaming routine.

There are, in addition, alarm systems which can be utilized in the sort of circumstance Marion Ludwig faced, and they are very effective. The same alarm systems that are designed to set off a wailing howl if a car thief tries to break into the car can be activated by a panic button device so that a woman, if she comes under attack or is frightened, can make a contact with her car which will set the alarm off. Again, in the face of a screaming alarm, the man who accosted Marion Ludwig would probably have run away.

I have one further suggestion. It's a little far out, but if readers will pay attention it could save their lives if and when they are under attack but can still get to their cars. The Morse code for SOS is short and simple to use: •••

— — — •••, three dots, three dashes, and three dots. Learn to tap that signal out on the horn of your car and it will summon help wherever you are. Most people know the signal, and it is far more effective to tap SOS out than to simply lie on the horn.

This procedure is also good to follow when family members are returning home after dark. If they are driving and, upon turning into the drive, see something that makes them nervous, they can tap out a signal, not necessarily an SOS, but a prearranged signal so that family members will know they need assistance.

Many families use such a system. It provides further assurance of ready help if and when needed. But just as important, it provides family members with an opportunity to talk about the daily hazards that exist around them. These discussions serve to keep children and parents alike more aware of and alert to procedures which, without being restrictive, can shield them against many hazards.

14

WALTER CARPENTER STARTED TOWARD the door of the office of his small insurance company. "I'll be away from my desk about forty-five minutes, Caroline," he told his wife.

Caroline Carpenter looked up from her desk. "All right, Walter, but don't be any longer. Remember, we have an appointment with Mr. Lambeth about that new air pilots policy."

Walter checked his wristwatch. "The Lambeth appointment is at eleven thirty, so I've got an hour. Plenty of time." He walked out onto the street, closing the door quietly behind him. It was a habit of his to turn and read with never-ending pride the gold lettering on a large window: "Walter and Caroline Carpenter. Insurance Brokers." They had been married over forty years and it had taken most of that time for them to build a business which kept them in comfort and allowed them to do things for their four children, all away from home, that all parents enjoyed doing.

It was the last week in November 1979. The weather in Memphis, Tennessee, was cool and crisp and Walter's light topcoat felt comfortable.

The bank where Walter had kept his business account for more than twenty years was eight blocks in a straight line from his office and he seldom drove his car when going there. He knew the walk would take fifteen minutes and, after making a deposit and checking his balance, fifteen minutes back. Walter, a meticulous man, liked to keep everything in proper order. In his business career there had never been such a thing as an overdrawn account.

Sherry Johnston looked up and smiled as Walter walked into the bank. "Good morning, Mr. Carpenter," she said cheerfully. "Seeing you each week is one of the nice things I can look forward to." Sherry brushed back her golden-blond hair; her bright blue eyes sparkled as they met Walter Carpenter's dark brown ones and refused to let them go.

Walter placed his small satchel of money on the counter. "That goes two ways, Sherry. I swear if they ever transfer you I'll take my banking business elsewhere. Tell that boss of yours it's about time they thought of moving you upstairs."

Sherry had been taking care of Mr. Carpenter's banking business for more than three years and the two were old friends....

The first shot slammed into a chandelier and sent fragments of glass showering down on waiting customers. The 12-gauge shotgun's roar spun Walter Carpenter around and froze Sherry Johnston to the high stool she was sitting on. Less than two hours before, she had read a bank association bulletin describing a team of bank bandits who had been plaguing Memphis-area institutions. She remembered the warning printed in large red letters: "THESE MEN ARE DANGEROUS AND MUST NOT BE RESISTED."

Now her heart almost stopped beating as the lead robber shouted, "Everybody flat on the floor with hands extended over your heads." The man's voice was harsh and frightening.

There were 16 customers waiting for service and bank personnel numbered 9, including the manager, Jack Lewis, and his assistant, Don Medford. There was also a uniformed, armed guard who was stationed during banking hours in the lobby's center where he sat behind a small desk. Jim Terril had guarded the bank for ten years. A retired Memphis police captain, he had celebrated his seventieth birthday in June and planned on retiring the first week in January 1980.

Jim was a pro, having spent his entire adult life in law enforcement on security work of some kind. He now sat with both hands on the desk top and looked impassively at the two bandits.

They were not young. He guessed them to be in their early forties and this told him that they were probably ex-cons. Both of them were armed with 12-gauge shotguns with sawed-off barrels which made them extremely deadly weapons. The men were both tall and slender. They moved like cats. Both wore stocking masks and their hands were covered with close-fitting brown kid gloves.

One of the bandits moved toward Jim and barked, "You lousy screw, hit the deck." He motioned with his gun.

Jim stood up. He was going to be real careful; the man's use of the term "screw" confirmed Jim's opinion that he was facing ex-cons—tough men who would brook no interference.

Terril moved out from behind the desk; he was going to lie down in front of it. The bandit either misunderstood his intentions or simply wanted to impress everyone else that they meant business. For whatever reason, he pulled the trigger of his weapon and heavy-gauge pellets nearly decapitated Jim Terril. He never knew what hit him. It is doubtful if he even heard the gun's roar.

The gunman who had killed Terril continued walking toward the service windows. "Your hands—keep them up in the air so I can see them." He approached Sherry Johnston's window and pulled a large cloth bag from his

118

pocket. "Fill it up, lady, every damned dollar you've got. Hold one back and it's bye-bye baby." He waved the shotgun in her face.

Walter Carpenter was lying on the floor directly in front of Sherry's window and the bandit had to step over him. Walter kept his face down with his cheek pressed hard against the flagstone floor. He was frightened and wanted no part of the gunmen.

Sherry scooped money out of her drawer and crammed it in the bag.

The bandit leaned over to be sure all the bills had been taken out of the drawer. He took the bag and backed away from Sherry's window. His heel caught Walter in the side and the bandit fell, sitting down backward with his legs bridging Walter.

The shotgun roared and Sherry fell with a gaping wound in her right shoulder.

Walter sat up and found himself face to face with the bandit, their legs entwined. The gun was pointed at Walter's chest and he grabbed the barrel, pushing it away.

The bandit rolled over and tore his gun from Walter's grasp. He sprang to his feet.

Walter Carpenter got to one knee: he was certain the man was going to shoot him.

The bandit pointed his weapon at Walter and pulled the trigger. The heavy pellets tore into Walter's left buttock and hip. The velocity of those shots slammed him down onto the stone floor. Walter remained conscious and, although he knew there was a bad wound, he felt no pain—only a numbness.

The second bandit, who had been standing back near the main entrance, ordered, "Come on, Buck, let's get out of here." Those orders saved Walter Carpenter's life. The gunman was already taking aim for a second shot with the barrel pointed at Walter's head. He hesitated a moment, then lowered his weapon and both bandits ran from the bank. Walter Carpenter thought he was dying.

The moment both bandits broke and ran, Jack Lewis, the manager, picked up a phone and called for paramedic services. They arrived in minutes.

When Walter saw the white jacket of a paramedic bending over him, he asked, "Sherry, is she all right?"

The paramedic nodded. "She'll make it, mister, and so will you."

Survival Techniques and Analysis

Walter Carpenter Case

Before getting into the issues and questions raised by this scenario, let me say that both Sherry and Walter did survive. This points up the first lesson of the case: Sherry Johnston and Walter Carpenter are alive today because the bank manager had insisted that all employees including himself post emergency numbers—including the paramedics'—in a spot where those numbers would be immediately available in case of an emergency. At the hospital, doctors said that if the paramedics had been as much as 60 seconds later in arriving at the scene, both Sherry and Walter would have died.

This basic item of emergency planning applies not only to banks and other institutions, but should be a cardinal rule in every home. Readers must understand that there are any number of situations where split seconds can make the difference between life and death: heart attacks, choking, bleeding, and accidental gunshot or knife wounds. If, when one of these emergencies occurs, people who are trying to help have to search for or look up emergency numbers, precious time is lost and victims can die. There is no excuse for not having emergency numbers posted directly on telephones so that not a single second is lost when time is precious.

Calling the operator in these circumstances is not acceptable. It takes too much time. Consider the time it takes to get an operator, then the explanation you have to give, and the fact that after all that the operator must place a call to the emergency service. If you have the emergency number available and place the call yourself, minutes are saved and those minutes or even seconds may save a life.

I'm going to repeat and emphasize this advice: *Post emergency numbers in large readable strips taped directly onto the telephone in your home and in your business office.* Do it now, even before you finish reading this chapter. We never know when an emergency can occur—perhaps in the next minutes or hours.

Having emergency numbers posted saved Walter Carpenter's life, but just barely. Walter did almost exactly what he should have done and still he was very nearly murdered. Chances are that if the bandit had not stumbled over Walter, he would never have been hurt nor would Sherry have been shot. The lesson here is that when dangerous conditions exist, anything can happen. Tensions generated by threatening and deadly circumstances cause people to become nervous and emotions can easily get out of hand. Walter Carpenter started off behaving correctly, and, had he continued to do so, he would not have been shot. When the bandit stumbled over Walter he should not have moved. Had he remained lying face down on the floor, there would have been no further shooting.

121

Readers must understand that in tense circumstances they must control their emotions and not perform sudden actions inspired by panic. I wonder how many people who read this chapter have given any thought to the possibility that they might be caught in the middle of a bank robbery. If so, has there been anything more than a passing speculation about what they would do? In today's atmosphere, the chances of facing such a situation are quite real, and we must all think about it and decide what must be done, in advance.

Once again, it's a matter of planning. Before making any move contrary to a robber's instructions, weigh carefully the consequences as they apply to each person being victimized. Don't become the trigger that sets off gunfire, agony, and death.

15

JOAN HATHAWAY WAS TIRED. She worked as a barmaid in the Red Turtle, a bar on Century Boulevard, just east of the Los Angeles International Airport. It was Friday and the crowds were big, bustling, and very often rude. Joan had been serving drinks since 6:00 p.m., and now it was 2:10 a.m. and the bar had shut down.

"Is that car of yours still acting up?" Joe Mendoza, a very heavyset bartender, asked Joan. "If it is, you'd better come home with me and not try the freeway at this time of the morning."

Joan was a good-looking woman. In her early forties, she worked hard at keeping a trim figure. Never married but often giving her favors to men who were kind to her, she was a free spirit and liked her own life-style, which included working around at different L.A. spots. Her jet-black hair, dark eyes, and brown complexion were a familiar sight to the late night and early morning crowd who got their relaxation and kicks out of making the rounds of several bars and meeting with old and new friends.

"I think it will be all right," she told Joe. "The damned thing is like a cranky woman. It runs fine for several hours, then suddenly starts to sputter and the engine stops. I've had it to the repair station twice and they can't find anything wrong."

"Sounds like a tankful of bad gas," Joe said, shaking his head. "There's been a lot of that since the shortage. You know we have an extra bedroom now that Joe Junior's moved out. Martha doesn't mind, she likes company."

"Not tonight, Joe. I'm too damned tired and I'm sure the car will make it home. It's only four-and-a-half miles." Joan slipped on a light raincoat. At the door she turned back. "It's raining cats and dogs. Be sure and put some towels under the back door or we'll be swamped in the morning."

"I'll take care of it," Joe answered and waved her out. "Get home safe and drive careful, hear?"

Joan drove her usual route west on Century for a few blocks; then she caught the on-ramp for the San Diego Freeway north toward Santa Monica. She would turn off on Robertson and be only three blocks from her apartment.

A quarter mile after she got on the freeway, the engine of her car began to sputter. Joan pumped the throttle and tried to coax it back to life. Suddenly it stopped and she coasted onto the shoulder and set the hand brake.

Rain slammed against the side of her 1971 Ford Mustang. A high wind was driving in from the Pacific Ocean. It was a Southern California storm dropping water by the bucketful.

Joan knew there was no emergency phone within a half mile, and the freeway seemed deserted.

Where the car came from she didn't know. Probably up the Venice Boulevard on-ramp. It seemed to Joan that it just appeared and slid in behind her. She recognized it as a Volkswagen van. Joan rolled the window of her Mustang down and heard a man's voice call out, "Can I be of any help?"

Joan Hathaway was not naive. She knew there was a chance a man could rape her, but under present circumstances who gave a damn? She'd slept with a man for less than a ride home. Besides, he might be very nice, she told herself.

Joan rolled the window up, opened the door, and stepped out. She took a moment to lock the Mustang and then ran back to the Volkswagen. The door on its passenger side flipped open and Joan ducked in and slammed the door behind her.

She looked at the driver. He was young, clean-shaven, and slender of build. There was no odor of alcohol about him. She smiled and sighed with relief. "Thanks for stopping. I was in one hell of a mess."

The man smiled back at her. His teeth were even and there was a dimple on one side. "Glad to help. Been there myself. Know what it feels like." He slipped the car in gear and drove around Joan's car. "I'm heading for Oxnard. Where do you go?" he asked Joan.

"I turn east on the Santa Monica Freeway and go a short distance to Robertson. I know it's out of your way, but I'll be glad to pay you."

"No need for that, lady. Why don't you just come to Oxnard with me. We'll sleep together and then I'll drive you back in the morning."

Joan sensed it wasn't a request but an order. "I'd rather not do that," she said firmly. "Why don't you just let me out where the Santa Monica Freeway intersects this one. I can walk the rest of the way."

He swung the Volkswagen over into the fast lane. "Nope, you're going to Oxnard with me." His foot pressed down on the throttle and the little car jumped ahead. "You're a good-looking gal, lady. A guy's got to grab it when it's available."

Joan hesitated a moment and then nodded her head. "I guess that's so. You won't be getting a cherry, mister. It could be lots more fun if you took a few minutes, drove to my place, and stayed there overnight."

"I hate a woman who gives it to me. More fun to take it. I tell you what, lady." He looked at her and there was no smile. "I'm going to beat the hell out of you. It'll hurt, but that's what makes me hot. I get stiff as a poker with a little blood."

Joan was frightened now and did not answer him.

They drove for more than a hour, neither of them saying anything. Just before they reached the city limits of Oxnard, the man swung his Volkswagen off the freeway onto a narrow paved road which he seemed to know.

"Where are we going now?" Joan asked.

He didn't answer but drove on for a few hundred yards, then pulled off on a wide shoulder and parked. He turned the engine off. "This is it, lady."

Joan did not hesitate for a moment now. She carried a nickel-plated .25 automatic in her purse, which was on the floor by her right foot. She leaned over, reached into the purse, and her hand wrapped around the small weapon's handle.

Joan straightened up and pointed the gun at the man. "Just a moment, buster," she said. "Start this car and take me into Oxnard or I'll blow a hole in you."

The man stared for a moment and then broke into a high-pitched laugh. "Go ahead, lady, pull the trigger. If you want to kill me over a piece of ass, let her go."

Joan didn't want to kill anyone. His reaction to the gun startled her. She had expected he would do as ordered in the face of her weapon. "I don't want to kill you," she murmured, "but you touch me and I'll shoot you."

The man's hand moved like a striking snake. Joan never stood a chance. He tore the gun from her grasp, turned it on her, and began firing. Five slugs hit her in the chest.

Joan Hathaway died with slugs from her own gun buried in her chest.

When the coroner completed his autopsy, he reported that she had been raped after death and that any one of the five shots would have been fatal.

Survival Techniques and Analysis

Joan Hathaway Case

Joan Hathaway's death and similar tragedies are all too familiar to people who live in Southern California. There have been six almost identical cases in the last two years. And yet people continue to ignore the warnings of common sense.

In Joan Hathaway's case, as in so many others, there seemed to be extenuating circumstances: the rain and wind; the absence of a nearby phone from which she could have summoned help. But none of these are valid excuses. Every freeway is patrolled by some law enforcement agency. While it's true that such patrols may not be frequent, it is far better to remain locked in one's own car until a properly authorized force arrives on the scene. You might have to wait for a number of hours. So what? At least you are alive, and the loss of a few hours cannot be compared to the value of your life.

This is exactly the advice given by most law enforcement agencies, but it is not popular or acceptable to many people. They would rather take a chance than wait for properly identified help to arrive. Once again, we have an example of the "I can take care of myself" or "it can't happen to me" syndrome.

Few people believe that such tragic events can occur in their lives. The purpose of *Survival* is to uncover the truth and destroy the myth. There is better than a 40 percent chance that one incident will occur in the life of every citizen unless he or she takes proper precautions to avoid circumstances which lead up to such crimes. It is a fact that the average man, woman, or child cannot take care of him or herself when faced with lethal violence. When someone is trying to kill you and has the means available to accomplish it, you do not have the emotional or physical training to fend off such an attack.

Joan Hathaway had prepared herself by carrying a gun and the man attacking was unarmed, and yet she was still unable to protect herself. Why?

A gun in the hands of one who is not properly trained in its use is worthless. In fact, as in the case of Joan Hathaway, it can be the means of death. Unless you have spent hours training in the art of handling handguns, *stay away from them.* They have the dangerous potential of lulling one into a sense of false security: the "I have a gun so no one can hurt me" syndrome. Even if one is properly trained, there are many people—particularly women—who, when faced with the necessity of dealing death from their own hand, find themselves incapable of pulling the trigger. They can't bring themselves to kill another human being. In addition to the manual training and dexterity required to handle a gun properly, there must be tough emotional training so that the specter of death leaping from the weapon in your hand does not become a barrier to using the weapon. That is probably what happened to Joan Hathaway. She could have shot her assailant, but didn't have the emotional make-up it took to pull the trigger.

Let me underscore the first basic rule to be gained from Joan's case: Do not accept a ride from a passing motorist, no matter how sane and solid such a person may seem. Thousands of people drive our freeways and highways every day; a breakdown or stall-out can happen to any of them.

If someone stops to offer help, tell him you want to remain with your car and ask him to get the nearest garage or service station to send help. Some states have standardized signals which tell passing motorists that a person needs help. A good one that everyone will recognize is to raise the hood of the car. If you are stalled after dark, raise the car's hood and get back in your car, lock its doors, and stay there until the patrol comes along or someone sends a tow truck to assist. You can roll the window down just enough to be able to talk to someone outside. If a motorist is sincerely trying to assist, he will do as you ask and send help. Do not let anyone talk you out of your car unless it is a person you recognize as a duly authorized service representative.

There have been cases in which a person was attacked when seated in a locked car. Often in such cases the windows have been smashed and the victim dragged bodily from the car. In such circumstances, a victim has little choice. There is going to be a physical confrontation. Usually, there is more than one assailant, and the victim is faced with several opponents, any of whom can kill. The first thing to remember is not to leave the protection of your car. Even if it becomes obvious that those attacking will eventually succeed in breaking in, make them do it. Make them drag you out. Time is in your favor. There is always a chance that the patrol will show up or another motorist will see what is happening and report it. Also remember that the modern automobile is not that easy to break into. The fact that a windshield is shattered or a window broken doesn't necessarily mean that the person on the outside is going to get in. People who drive the highways a lot should carry some sort of a weapon in the car. Not necessarily a gun, but some sort of canister, Mace, tear gas, or one of the other products on the market. With about three hours of training in California, you can be licensed to carry and use such weapons. If someone is trying to break into your car, they can be very effective.

129

Equipping a car with a citizens band radio is also a good idea. A call for help with such a radio can bring fast results. Many modern law enforcement agencies monitor these frequencies on a 24-hour basis.

There is also the possibility of using a panic button. There are alarm systems designed for installation in cars. They can be set so that if there is an attempt made to enter the car during the owner's absence, they will trigger and make a god-awful screaming sound which can be heard for miles. The alarm can also be connected to a panic button on the inside of the car so that a person locked inside and under attack can hit the button and the alarm will sound. Even if you are under attack from several people and they are beating on the car and smashing windows, the alarm can bring fast help. The assailants know this and may very well be frightened away. It's true they can smash the alarm, but that will take time and even a few blasts may bring the help you need.

One more very important point is that Joan was driving a car which she knew was not reliable. If you are going to drive freeways at night, be certain that your automobile is in good shape—engine, tires, cooling system, etc. People must understand that on the freeways, unlike travel at surface street level, there are long lonely stretches where, if a car breaks down, its occupants are faced with dangerous exposure in long walks, sometimes miles. One final precaution. If you are going to travel a freeway at night, let someone know which freeway and when you expect to arrive home. I know that is not always possible, but when it is, do it. If you are overdue because of a breakdown, the person expecting you can start a search and quickly locate you. Remember, prevention is the name of the game. Do what you can within reason to avoid dangerous circumstances and most of the game is won.

16

DECEMBER 1979, PHOENIX, ARIZONA. It was three days before Christmas and Hank Donahue was in a hurry to get home. A senior student of Mining and Engineering at the Colorado School of Mines in Golden, Hank had delayed coming home for his Christmas vacation. He had wanted to spend some days with his roommate, Charles Castle, in Grand Junction, a small city in western Colorado. His parents had expected him the day before and he knew they would be disappointed.

The speedometer of Hank's 1973 Mercury held steady at 55 miles per hour. A long straight segment of road leading into Phoenix from the east had a tendency to lull drivers into a doze, particularly if they had been driving for many hours.

Hank was driving directly into the sun setting low on the western horizon. His tired eyes succumbed to weariness and strain and their lids began to close.

Then it happened. The windshield of Hank's car dissolved into a curtain of flying glass spray. Sharp crystal-hard particles of shattered glass cut Hank's face in dozens of places. Blood oozed from tiny cuts and particles of glass remained stuck in his flesh.

Hank slammed on the brakes, and as the car skidded to a sliding stop, he opened the door on his side and stepped out. "What the hell did I hit?" he asked himself.

The answer came quickly. Hank heard the ugly snarl of a high-powered rifle and a metallic crash as a heavy lead slug smashed through the right-hand door.

An 18-wheeler traveling in the opposite direction came to a halt alongside Hank's car. The driver leaned out the window and called, "Got a problem, mister?"

Before Hank could answer, the rifle roared again and the truck driver saw a hole suddenly appear in the hood of his diesel tractor. "Get the hell out of here, mister," he shouted. "Some crazy bastard is shooting at us." He slammed the truck into gear and moved out fast.

Hank Donahue jumped back into the Merc and floor-boarded the throttle. As he sped away he noticed several small hillocks to his right and assumed the shots were coming from that direction. He didn't see a car or person but noticed there were several dirt roads leading off the main highway toward the hillocks.

About five miles west of where the attack had occurred, Hank caught up with a highway patrol unit and flagged them down.

Officer Larry Parks hollered to his partner, "Tim! Look over here. The guy's trying to wave us down. Looks like he's run into our sniper."

Tim Barrington took one look at Hank's bleeding face and the fractured windshield of his car and ordered, "Stop, Larry. That man's hurt. You're right—that damned sniper is at it again."

Three minutes later Hank was pouring out his story to the two patrolmen. He was interrupted by the officers' radio: "Sniper reported on Highway 66 about twenty miles east of city limits. Report comes from a truck driver whose rig was hit. He reports that another car was involved traveling west and the driver of that car was cut about the face."

Officer Barrington turned to Hank and asked, "Can you tell us exactly where the shots were fired?"

Hank nodded. "I checked the distance on my odometer. It's exactly five and three-tenths of a mile back of where we are now. Look, officer, I can take you there."

Officer Parks was on the radio. "We've got the other victim. His face is badly cut and I'm driving him into the hospital. Tim will take our unit and head for the sniping area. This victim pinpoints the rolling mesa area. All traffic moving east or west from that area should be stopped."

There was a minute's silence; then the radio crackled: "Roadblocks are being placed now. Your information jibes with that of the truck driver's. Other units will be there when you arrive. Can you furnish the name of your victim?"

Larry Parks gave headquarters Hank's full name and the hospital he was being transported to.

Hank Donahue sat back in the front passenger seat of his Mercury and closed his eyes. He could hear Officer Parks's voice over the sound of wind coming through the broken windshield. "You were very lucky. That rifle slug is buried right behind your head in the backseat cushion. How it missed you was a miracle."

Hank's face was beginning to hurt. He thought of his home, his parents, and his plans for after graduation. Why had someone tried to kill him? How could he or anyone else survive when, for no reason, they could become targets for a man and his rifle?

Survival Techniques and Analysis

Hank Donahue Case

Indeed, how can anyone shield himself against a sense-less attack launched at random by a mentally deranged person?

I'm not sure there are any positive or easy answers to that question. This sort of unprovoked attack occurs more often than anyone likes to admit: during the last two years the incidence has more than doubled. It is a circumstance we all may have to face, and therefore *Survival* must address the facts and offer the best protective shields available.

First of all, there was no way for Hank Donahue to have avoided the sniper's attack. In that sort of situation he had no chance to see, hear, or even get a hunch about the possibility of a sniper.

However, once the attack began, Hank might have acted differently. Because of his drowsy condition just before the attack, he probably did not know what had struck his windshield. That's why he stopped. If he had heard a shot and connected it with his shattered windshield, he should not have stopped. Rule number one should be: The instant you recognize that you are a target, get out! Drive away or run away as quickly as possible. If, for some reason, running is not possible either by vehicle or on foot, *take cover*.

The sniping attack that occurred in 1961 on a university campus in Austin, Texas, brings up another important issue. Fifteen people were killed and 31 wounded by a man shooting from a tower on the campus. Some experts felt that the victims' reactions were slowed down by the fact that they were not absolutely sure where the shots were coming from. The question naturally arises: Until you are sure of where shots are coming from, how can you run or take cover?

Experts disagree. Some say that to run or try to take cover before locating the exact place a sniper is shooting from can be extremely dangerous. A victim may run or drive directly toward a sniper without realizing it. The opposing opinion is based on the fact that a moving target is much harder to hit than a stationary one. If you are driving in a car and you become aware that someone is shooting at you, you don't have many options. Either keep driving at the same rate of speed you were using when hit; or stop, get out, and try to locate the sniper; or finally, floorboard the throttle and get the hell out of there as fast as the car will go.

I support the last choice. You will recall that after the assassination of President Kennedy, one of the strongest grounds for disbelieving the Warren Commission's conclusions was the difficulty inherent in hitting a moving target with such accuracy.

The problem is different for a person on foot, but my advice is the same. Get the hell out of there as fast as you can. If you are running from a shooting sniper, incorporate "evasive action." Don't run in a straight line, but zigzag, making an evasive turn with every other step. Crouch low, close to the ground, and if the attack occurs in daylight, head for shadows. But whatever you do, *run*. Don't stand and give a sniper a chance for a second shot at a stationary target.

Let's go back to the sniper attack on an automobile. What should a person do if the sniper's first shot disables the vehicle? Or if the driver is injured so badly that he or she can no longer drive?

Keep in mind that the automobile offers a fair degree of protection. While it's true that a high-powered rifle will penetrate the metal skin of your car if the range is close enough, it is also true that after such penetration the slug has slowed down to such a degree that it will do far less damage to the human body. If for any reason a victim cannot drive away from the shooting scene, he should crouch down in his car, get below the window level, and roll up in a tiny ball to reduce the chance of a slug coming through the car and striking him. The sniper will probably not take more than two or three shots before he leaves. The chances of his approaching the car are nil. He doesn't want to be caught, so, if given a chance, he'll get out.

The psychology of sniping raises a number of interesting, if difficult, questions. What makes a man take up a weapon and start to fire, seemingly at random, at people he has never seen before?

There are several theories. One school of thought connects sniping with the frustrations and emotional pressures of our modern society. Certain people, this school argues, cannot tolerate these pressures, and at some point they crack, striking out in anger, trying to hurt other people or the world in general. It is their answer to nagging problems for which they can find no solution.

Another school of thought attributes certain types of sniper activity, usually where the victims are women, to some sort of sexual aberration. Experts have written at length about stabbers of young women. There are hundreds of such attacks each year, where men stab with small knives, long pins, and almost every conceivable kind of stabbing instrument. In such cases, the assailant actually reaches sexual climax. Ejaculation occurs at the moment the weapon penetrates a victim's flesh.

A case cited by Richard von Krafft-Ebing, a nineteenth-century neurologist, demonstrates this type of aberration:

Bartle the wine merchant was subject to lively sexual excitement at the age of fourteen, though decidedly opposed to its satisfaction by coitus, his aversion going so far as disgust for the female sex. At that time, he already had the idea to cut girls, and thus satisfy his sexual desire. He refrained from it, however, because of lack of opportunity and courage. He disdained masturbation, but now and then had "pollutions" with erotic dreams of girls who had been cut. At the age of nineteen, he cut a girl for the first time. During the act he had a seminal emission and experienced intense pleasure.

From that time the impulse grew constantly more powerful. He chose only young and pretty girls and, as a rule, asked them before the deed whether they were still single. The ejaculation or sexual satisfaction occurred only when he was sure that he had actually wounded the girls. After such an act he always felt tired and bad, and was also troubled with qualms of conscience.

Up to his thirty-second year, he pursued this process of cutting but was careful not to wound the girls dangerously. From that time until his thirty-sixth year, he was able to control his impulse. Then he sought to satisfy himself by simply pressing the girls on the arm or neck, but this gave rise to erections only and not to ejaculation. Then he sought to attain his object by pricking the girls with the knife left in its sheath, but this did not suffice. Finally he stabbed with the open knife and had complete success. For he thought that a girl stabbed bled more and suffered more pain than when merely cut.

In his thirty-seventh year he was detected and arrested. In his lodgings was found a collection of daggers, sword canes, and knives. He said that the mere sight of these weapons, and still more, the grasping of them, gave him an intense feeling of sexual pleasure, with violent excitement. According to his own confession, he had injured fifty girls in all. His external appearance was rather pleasing. He lived in very good circumstances, but was peculiar and shy.

This bizarre nineteenth-century case may well shed some light on the psychology of today's snipers. The theory has been expounded that the sniper suffers from the same aberration as the stabber—but the sniper obtains his sexual thrill by "stabbing" his victims from a distance, using a rifle instead of a knife. There are a number of cases on file that seem to support this possibility.

It should be added that the chance of becoming a sniper's target is still so remote that there is no need for altering one's style of living in order to avoid the risk. Your chances of being hurt in an automobile accident are very much greater than of being selected at random by a sniper. Maybe the soundest advice I can offer in *Survival* is not to be frightened by the occasional reporting of such attacks.

17

WASHINGTON, D.C., DECEMBER 11, 1979. Dorothy Carroll, 28, nearly six feet tall with a slender high-fashion model's figure, was crying. Tears streamed down her cheeks and it seemed her large brown eyes would dissolve in puddles. "There isn't anything more I can do, Paul," Dorothy said in a broken voice. "I've been to the police, the courts, and to you—my attorney. In spite of the court order restraining him from bothering me, David persists and I'm afraid. He keeps saying he will kill me."

Paul Carter shook his head. "I know how you must feel, Dorothy," he said in a soothing voice, "but believe me, there is nothing else anyone can do until David pulls something which will give authorities jurisdiction." Paul Carter, twenty years Dorothy's senior, was gray and partly bald. A good attorney, he had been practicing for twenty years in the Washington area, specializing in marital cases. "You were married to David for more than twelve years. During that period did he ever display violent behavior which would lead you to believe he could commit murder?"

Dorothy shook her head. "No. He was never violent toward me. David was extremely jealous and on occasions would threaten to fight another man who he thought was too attentive to me. But it was all sham. I don't know what he would have done if an actual confrontation had taken place."

"I remember, in your divorce action, you charged David with constant infidelity. The fact that he felt free to run around with other women didn't change his possessive attitude toward you?"

"Not at all," Dorothy replied. "Right now I don't believe he wants me back, but he is determined that no other man shall become interested in me. As you know, he watches my place constantly and if another man shows up, David does something to interrupt any plans we might have. He gets very ugly, threatening to kill me and anyone I'm with."

Paul got to his feet and walked out around the large oaken desk. "I've got a court appearance at eleven, Dorothy, and I have to leave." He looked at his watch. "It's ten thirty; there isn't much time." He walked with her to the door. "Keep in touch, and at the slightest sign of David's harming you, get in contact with my office. They will always be able to locate me."

Dorothy wiped her eyes with a white linen handkerchief. "I'm really frightened, Paul. If only there was some way I could leave Washington and make a new life somewhere else. But I have a good position here and then there's the property—it would take time to dispose of my condo. I have your home number. Do you mind if I call you during the evening?"

"Not at all, Dorothy. Call anytime you feel nervous. That's why I gave you my home number."

It was past noon when Dorothy arrived home. She lived in Rockville, Maryland, a 45-minute drive from downtown Washington.

Lawrence and Bell Harrington had been neighbors of the Carrols' for ten years. They were sorry to see Dorothy and David break up, but the Carrols' marriage had been in trouble for several years. The couple had no children, and to a great degree had found separate interests. David had a fine position in the stock market and spent several days each week in New York. It was during these trips that he would get involved with other women. Dorothy worked on Capitol Hill as secretary for a senior senator. Dorothy and David were considered to be smart, sophisticated people, entirely capable of handling a divorce situation, but Dorothy was finding that things were not working out as she had planned.

Bell Harrington met Dorothy in the underground garage. She had been waiting there for some time and seemed nervous. "Dorothy," she said as soon as the young women got out of her car, "I just had to come down and warn you. David has been here several times this morning and seems to be very upset. You know he still has his keys to your place and there's no telling what he might do."

Dorothy took Bell's arm. "It was nice of you to take the trouble, Bell," she said firmly. "I had expected David this afternoon. We made arrangements to meet in order to straighten out our property settlement. I have no idea why he should have been upset this morning."

The two women walked together toward an elevator. As they neared the sliding door, a man stepped out from behind a parked car.

His voice was grinding and harsh as he called out, "Dorothy!"

Dorothy spun around. The man was no more than five feet from her. "David!" she cried. "What are you doing here? We were to meet this afternoon."

"I decided to change the time. Where have you been?" he demanded.

"It's none of your business—but I don't mind telling you. I spent the morning with Paul Carter; we were discussing the property settlement among other things."

141

David moved closer. "I've decided how the property settlement is going to be handled, and that shyster attorney isn't going to have a damned thing to do with it."

Bell Harrington tugged at Dorothy's arm. "Come on, Dorothy, don't argue with him. Let the attorneys and the court handle it." Then she saw the revolver in David's hand. "My God!" she screamed. "Dorothy—David has a gun in his hand."

Dorothy pulled her arm away from Bell. "You go on up, Bell. David and I can settle our differences better if we are alone."

David interrupted. "Stay where you are, Bell. You had a part in this whole damned thing. Don't think I'm ignorant of the many times you advised Dorothy to leave me."

"All right, David," Bell said with mounting anger, "I'll admit I did. You weren't good enough for Dorothy. I've said it many times and there's no reason for me to change my opinion now."

"I'm going to give you a good reason right now." David raised the revolver and pointed it at Bell. "There's one way to stop that goddamned nasty tongue of yours."

Dorothy was scared. She screamed, "David! Put that gun down. Bell didn't have anything to do with my leaving you."

David's voice was high-pitched, on the verge of hysteria. "You're a liar. You always were." Then he pulled the trigger and the .38 police special roared. Bell Harrington died instantly with a lead slug in her brain.

Dorothy backed away. "Good God, David," she cried in shocked disbelief. "You've killed her."

David nodded. "You're damned right. She deserved it and you're next." He turned the revolver toward Dorothy and fired. The bullet caught her on the left side of her chest and tore a large chunk from her heart. Dorothy Carrol never felt herself hit the pavement: she was killed instantly.

For a moment David Carrol looked at the two women; then, without saying a word, he put the revolver to his own head and pulled the trigger.

Three people died that morning because, in the words of the homicide investigator, "No one understood the dynamics of murder."

Survival Techniques and Analysis

Dorothy Carrol Case

In *Survival* I have dealt with a large number of crimes that have ended in murder, but most of the crimes were not murder cases. The distinction is important, both for crime prevention and for the police investigating a crime. Where there is a basic crime—such as robbery, burglary, assault, extortion, or rape—that ends in a killing, there may be a felony murder conviction, but the basic crime is not murder. If during an armed robbery a victim is shot and killed, the investigation of that crime is assigned to the robbery squad, not to homicide. Investigative techniques will be geared toward robbery, isolating the kind of establishment being hit by the robbers, selecting likely future victims, and setting up stakeouts at appropriate sites.

In the basic crime of murder, there are no motivating factors to support other crimes. In Dorothy Carrol's case, there was no attempt to rob or rape. David had only one intent: to kill. Even his self-destruction was an extension of his murderous intent.

Readers should understand that any man or woman can, if emotional circumstances provide sufficient motive, become a killer. Crime statistics show that a large percentage of murders arise from serious conflict between family members.

It is difficult for any of us to understand that a person we have known and perhaps, like Dorothy Carrol, lived with for many years, can become so emotionally upset that he or she will kill us. Most victims of murder are people who would swear that such a thing could not possibly happen to them.

The primary lesson of Dorothy Carrol's case, then, is that every person is capable of murder.

The law in most states recognizes this concept. Temporary insanity has long been an acceptable defense in murder trials. Second-degree murder, defined as killing motivated by sudden emotional passions, is a part of the body of law in many states.

We must all understand our limits in withstanding emotional trauma and have some feeling for the depth of agony that those we love can tolerate. It doesn't make any difference how kind, considerate, and dear to us the other party may have been: we must recognize the change and defend ourselves against the possibility of murder.

Dorothy Carrol was trying to do just that when she talked with her attorney. Her words were "I'm very frightened and would leave Washington if it were possible." She sensed the danger but did not understand how to protect herself against it.

Unfortunately, law enforcement agencies cannot handle such matters until there has been some overt act committed that seriously threatens the life of a complainant. Attorneys can go into court and get all sorts of restraining orders, but they are of little value: if the person restrained has murder in mind, he or she couldn't care less about a contempt charge after murder has been committed. Thus the threatened party must take realistic and positive action to protect him or herself.

Dorothy Carrol confronted a very difficult situation in trying to protect herself against her ex-husband. Even a good bodyguard could not have protected her against David's sudden attack. The first step a probable victim should take is to sever completely any relationship with the disturbed party. It may be only temporary, but the threatened person should leave the immediate area and take positive steps to be certain the disturbed party does not know where he or she is. This disappearance must continue until there has been sufficient cooling-off time to allow the disturbed person to reconsider the finality of his contemplated act.

Dorothy had arranged a meeting for that afternoon with the man she was afraid of, although property settlements and any other business concerning David could have been handled by her attorney. Dorothy was inviting trouble when she continued to have physical contact with David. She should have been off the scene. I know how difficult a disappearing act can be, what with jobs, children, and school. But dead is for a long time. The difficulty of arranging for a short disappearance is a cheap price to pay for one's life.

If a person cannot disappear, then Dorothy's procedure should be followed up to a point. Have an attorney seek the proper restraining orders from local courts. Report your concern to the local law enforcement agency, keeping in mind that it has certain legal limitations. Stay as far away as possible from the threatening person. Never meet him or her alone; make certain your appointments take place in the office of your attorney. If the person who is threatening should suddenly appear, as in Dorothy's case, understand the danger and act accordingly. Do not antagonize the person further. Do not remind him or her of any restraining court order you have obtained. Make no move and speak no word which may drive the person over the edge. If you have some understanding of the person's emotional problem, it may be possible to carefully move him or her back from the brink. You have read about potential suicides poised on the ledges of high buildings and how they have been saved by people who understood their emotional makeup.

Handle the situation as you would handle a time bomb. Slow, careful, no panic. Remember, you have a capacity to reason, to think, to seek an answer no matter the circumstance. The presence of a person threatening to kill you—even if that person displays the ready means of committing that act, such as a gun or knife—does not present an impossible situation. Your understanding of the person and your capacity to handle a difficult situation can save your life.

18

APRIL 1979, INGLEWOOD, CALIFORNIA. It was a soft balmy night with California's spring moon full and round and yellow. West of the city were the Palos Verdes Hills, overlooking the rocky coast between Marina Del Rey and Long Beach.

A scenic road ran along the bluff's top and there were turn-off spots which offered unobstructed views of the Pacific Ocean. These spots were favorite parking places for young people seeking a place to be alone and indulge their romantic inclinations.

It was 1:30 a.m. Tom Lansing, twenty-one, and his date Louise Galken, eighteen, sat in Tom's 1973 Dodge van. They had been dating for more than a year and every Friday night it was dinner, dancing, and a few moments for intimate talk and making love in some secluded spot.

Louise pushed Tom back. "I really didn't want to come here tonight, Tom. It's very frightening; we've both read about the stocking cap rapist attacking young couples right around here."

Tom laughed. "Don't worry about him, honey. If he shows, I know how to take care of him." Tom reached across Louise's lap and opened the glove compartment of his car. "Look what's in there and stop worrying."

Louise recognized the checkered handle of a snub-nosed revolver. "Isn't that illegal? Don't you have to have some sort of a permit to carry a weapon in the car?"

"Sure, but who's going to know it? Permit or no permit, I'm carrying a gun when I'm out at night. If the police can't protect us we've got a right to take care of ourselves."

Louise shuddered. "You know I'm not ordinarily nervous about such things, but it seems to me we're taking an unnecessary risk. Now the gun. You shouldn't have it, Tom, not unless you've got a proper permit."

Tom took his arm from around her shoulder. "OK, Louise, let's go. I just didn't like the idea of having some creep drive us away from our favorite spot."

Louise touched him on his arm. "That creep, according to the newspaper reports, has a gun and isn't afraid to use it. Do you realize we are the only car parked here? Other men are more concerned than you are."

Tom leaned forward and turned the key.

"Hold it right there, friend." The voice was low and threatening.

Tom look up and saw a .45 automatic pointed at his head. "Be careful with that gun, mister," Tom said. "I don't want to get shot."

Louise was paralyzed with fear. She couldn't speak. The stranger was tall and black, with a slender build and a small mustache. She remembered the description printed in the local newspapers. The man standing next to Tom fit every detail.

The gunman opened Tom's door. "Get out, and hold your hands in back of you," he ordered. Louise's date stepped out of the car. She sensed he might put up some sort of resistance and prayed that he wouldn't.

"Now, lady, you slide over here and get out." The man motioned with his gun.

148

When Louise got out of the car, he handed her a three-foot piece of quarter-inch rope. "Tie your friend's hands behind his back. I'll check it. If it isn't a good job, he's a goner. I'll kill him."

Tom stood with his back to Louise. He clasped his hands together in back of him. "Tie it tight, honey," Tom whispered. "I believe the man means what he says."

Louise worked slowly. She remembered the stories of other victims. In each case the rapist had tied the man and then attacked the girl. On one occasion when the girl's date objected too vigorously, the gunman shot him.

"Hurry it up, lady, I haven't got all night," the black man said with growing irritation.

Tom wanted to tell Louise to bide her time and get the gun in the glove compartment, but there was no chance. He winced as Louise pulled the rope tight.

Finally she was finished. "His hands are bound tight," she told the gunman. "There is no chance for him to free himself."

The gunman stepped forward and tested her tying job. He pulled at the rope but was unable to undo it. "That's good. Now, mister, lie down on the ground and keep your mouth shut. Don't move a finger if you want to stay alive." Even though he was speaking through a tight silk stocking mask which covered his entire face and head, Tom could understand him. Tom dropped to his knees and then forward onto his face. He kept quiet.

"Into the back seat, honey," the gunman ordered. "You and I are going to have a party." He opened the back door of Tom's van, and murmured, "Wouldn't it be nice if there was a bed inside?"

Louise moved toward the van. "There is," she spoke up. She had made up her mind to cooperate. There was no choice.

149

Inside the van the gunman put the weapon in his right-hand pocket. He grabbed at Louise and tore at her upper clothing.

"There's no need to hurt me," she protested. "I'll give you whatever you want. Give me a chance to enjoy it with you."

The man's fist smashed into her face and she staggered back against the van's metal side. "Knock off the bullshit, lady," the man hissed. "You're so goddamned scared, there's no way you could enjoy a piece of ass. That's the way I like it, lady." He grabbed her and bit her bared breast hard.

Louise screamed, "My God! Are you trying to kill me?"

Tom heard her cry and struggled against the rope binding his hands.

Forty-five minutes later, the gunman opened the van's back door and climbed out. He walked over to where Tom was lying. "She was a good piece of ass after I knocked some fight into her," he said in an even tone of voice. "Don't worry, she'll get over it—but it's gonna take some time. Pretty well bruised up."

Tom did not answer. He had rolled onto his back and he watched the gunman walk away and disappear into the night.

Tom then struggled to his feet and walked to the open van. What he saw made him sick. Louise was stretched out on the mattress bed. She looked as though a truck had collided with her. Both eyes were black and her nose was flat. One breast was bleeding and there was a series of bites around her lower belly. She was conscious. Her eyes found his. "The gun, Tom," she gasped. "The gun. Get it and kill me."

Survival Techniques and Analysis

Louise Galken Case

The lesson of this case is *not* that young people should stop "parking." They've been doing that since the beginning of recorded history, and I'm sure they're going to continue doing it. It's not parking I'm objecting to, but parking in a stupid place. Don't ask for trouble—that's the number one lesson to learn from this case.

Tom Lansing had a responsibility to take care of Louise which began when he asked her to go out with him. She had a right to expect that he would not deliberately expose her to any extraordinary hazards. Just before the gunman appeared, she expressed her displeasure with the situation. Tom ignored all precepts of common sense when he drove them to the very area where there had been substantiated reports of shootings and rapes. There is little doubt that he thought the gun in the glove compartment provided all the protection he and Louise would need. A perfect example of the dangers of keeping a weapon handy unless you understand its use and limitations. The presence of a gun can impart a false sense of security that can lead a person to challenge circumstances he would otherwise not think of confronting.

Some readers might find my insistence on a man's responsibility to protect a woman he asks out a bit Victorian, but I don't think that's fair. Young and old alike must accept a concept that I believe is inherent in the very nature of the man/woman relationship. Costs can be divided on a date, a woman can ask a man for his company, and I am sure there are other customs that will change as time passes. But the male's protector role will remain. When a man and a woman share company, she has a right to expect that in the event of danger her male escort will do whatever is necessary to protect her, even to the point of sacrificing his life. In the case we are discussing, there is no evidence to support a theory that Tom did not want to protect Louise. He simply did not have any chance to do so. Here is an important point I want to stress. To needlessly sacrifice one's life in a grand heroic gesture is nonsense. It is the ultimate display of selfish self-image adoration. When a man is faced with a situation that threatens his woman companion, he must know his own limitations and conduct himself within those bounds.

When Tom found it impossible to get to his weapon, he realized that resistance would result in his own death and possibly that of Louise, so he capitulated. Tom had no capability to handle the situation he faced without his gun; and because he was not trained in its use, even if he had managed to get to it, the chances are that the gunman would have killed him and Louise.

Now I am going to undertake what is probably the most difficult part of my argument in *Survival*. In the society we live in, our educational process must train our young people in the art of self-defense. I don't mean that every boy and girl should become a black-belt titlist, but there should be a required minimum degree of proficiency in the art of protecting oneself against attack.

I acknowledge that there are difficulties in indiscriminate teaching of certain techniques. We need to properly train children to face the challenges of the eighties; but it would be dangerous and foolish to teach protective techniques to the bad guys as well as the good ones. That problem has been recognized since the beginning of martial arts. In the Far East, where such arts were developed, they would not be taught to anyone without a long initial period of observation and close physical contact. If a person's character did not meet standards that would allow him or her to have and exercise the arts without endangering the rest of society, that person would be dropped from a class. The same reasoning restrains me from including in *Survival* a detailed discussion of proper and positive techniques of self-protection.

Those who agree that our young people ought to be properly trained in self-defense should therefore seek out private instruction. Parents who are interested in providing such schooling for their children, or adults who feel the need for such instruction, must select a training facility within their community that will satisfy their needs.

Such training courses can only be found now in large metropolitan areas, but I have a proposed solution for this difficulty. Every community has a law enforcement agency, either local, county, state, or federal. The majority of these agencies have officers who have been well trained in the art of self-defense. If a sensible program is conceived which would bring together the local law enforcement agency and concerned parents, I am sure the agency could provide the teaching talent to conduct classes in a semiprivate surrounding. Participants in these classes should be well screened so that dangerous knowledge is not placed in the hands of those who would abuse it.

There might be some problem with involving a public agency in that sort of a limited program. However, the trained officers could take the project on as a private enterprise and charge a small fee. Then they could set reasonable requirements for student participation.

Even if we assume that Tom and Louise were totally unprepared for attack, there is still something they might have done to protect themselves. Most such attacks take place after dark. The accurate use of a handgun, especially in the dark, requires weeks and months of intensive training. Most people, including rapists, have not devoted such time and effort to proficiency in the use of their weapons. If, when ordered out of the car, Tom had instantly run, it is probable that the rapist could not have hit him with a bullet. At the same time, if Louise had opened the door on the car's opposite side and run, the rapist wouldn't have known which way to go. Both Louise and Tom would, at this time, have represented a very real danger to him.

This sort of action would require a coordinated plan on the part of Louise and Tom; but I am convinced that there isn't anything wrong with couples preplanning escape action. This goes back to the basic concept of *Survival*. Anyone who wants to live a productive and long life in the American society of the 1980s must recognize the hazards that society poses. Once one admits the presence of such dangers, then it follows logically that one should take ordinary precautions to avoid situations that are hazardous and to plan one's protection in the event of danger.

If Tom had decided to resist but was untrained in the art of self-protection, then running would be his safest choice. He should run as low to the ground as possible and not in a straight line, but take evasive twists and turns with each step.

On the other hand, if Tom, as he did, decided to let matters take their course, Louise might have gotten out the other side of the car and made a run for it herself.

There's nothing wrong with that course of action as far as Louise is concerned, but there is a good chance such an action would have cost Tom his life. Where two people are involved, a preplanned coordinated action is a must unless one of them doesn't care about what happens to the other. For either Louise or Tom to have run without warning the other would have left the one who remained at the mercy of an enraged gunman.

Once Tom was tied up and Louise was faced with the fact that an armed man was going to rape her, the situation became even tougher. Running was no longer a good idea. Tom was disposed of and the rapist could easily have chased Louise and would probably have caught her. She might have faked a seizure or heart attack or just fainted, but even this, I'm afraid, might not have helped much. A fake seizure or fainting is effective primarily in cases where the assailant wants money more than anything else. This gunman could easily have taken Tom's wallet, which had several hundred dollars in it, when he was finished with Louise; but he wasn't interested. He was a rapist; once Louise was in his power, he wouldn't have cared what shape she was in. It is true that raping an unconscious woman is extremely difficult; but it's likely that this rapist would have beaten Louise, perhaps to death, had she faked a fainting spell. Don't forget that violence is part of the true rapist's foreplay.

Louise Galken recognized that there were no further options open to her, and she opted to stay alive.

19

JULY 1979, YELLOWSTONE PARK. Dorothy Pearlman laughed. "I never was considered much of a cook at home where everything was available. But trying to make a meal over a campfire, half blinded by smoke and with two burned hands—I give up." She backed away from the smoldering fire, carrying a frying pan sizzling with bacon and eggs with her.

David, her husband of less than a year, came to the rescue. "Here, let me have that," he said gently. He took the frying pan from her hand and set it down on a flat sandstone rock. He looked fondly at his wife. Dorothy was thirty-one years old, a pretty natural blonde, her hair cut in a short sculptured bob that framed her freckled face. Big blue eyes separated by a turned-up pug nose were squinted shut and tears ran down each cheek in protest at the acrid wood smoke. Dorothy was scarecrow thin and, although doctors had told her she was perfectly healthy, it seemed impossible for her to put on weight.

Her husband handed her a big bandanna. She wiped each eye and squinted at him. "I guess I'm not the outdoor type, honey. The trees and mountains and lakes are all very lovely. But come nighttime, I feel much happier and safer in my own little apartment on Fifth Avenue. As for the animals, I can see plenty of them in the zoo just a few blocks away in Central Park."

"OK, dear," David responded. "Maybe it was a mistake to try and transplant you even for a couple of weeks. This is the kind of country I grew up in—the Colorado Rockies. When I was a youngster I camped out nearly all summer long. Montrose was just a few miles from some virgin mountain country. My favorite spot was much wilder than this. A place called Buck-horn Lake. You could only get to it by packhorse." David was ten years older than Dorothy. They matched each other in height—both were five feet ten inches—but there all similarity stopped. David had a mop of shiny black curly hair and his dark brown eyes and heavy features hinted of Slavic or possibly Arabic ancestry. He had graduated from the school of mining engineering at Golden, Colorado, and taken a position with a firm in New York. He first met Dorothy when she was hired as his secretary; three years later they were married.

He took her in his arms. "We'll move into the lodge tomorrow night. To tell the truth, I'm getting a little sick of the rugged life. Those sleeping bags aren't that comfortable."

Dorothy bent over and started to pick up the frying pan. "Well, it's back to the open fire if we're going to have any supper."

Again David took the frying pan from her hand and placed it on the flat rock. "Leave it there, honey," he said. "You and I are going over to the lodge. We'll make reservations for tomorrow night and then have a good dinner in their dining room."

"That sounds good to me." She gave him a quick little hug. "You should have married one of your mountain girls rather than a dyed-in-the-wool, born-and-bred New Yorker."

The sun was setting when they left for the thirty-minute drive to Yellowstone Lodge. In their hurry to get on their way, they had left the frying pan and half-cooked meal on the flat rock. Neither of them remembered the ranger's warning not to leave food anywhere unprotected from the forage of the park's many wild animals.

It was past ten o'clock when David and Dorothy returned to their camping spot. It took them only a few minutes to disrobe in their car and roll out sleeping bags side by side near the still smoldering fire.

Their sleeping bags were about two feet apart. Dorothy rolled over and touched his hand. "Thanks for being considerate, darling. I love being your wife, but it's nice to know this is my last night playing the part of Pocahontas."

Dorothy and David went to sleep undisturbed. Later, in his conversation with the chief park ranger, David thought it was about an hour before dawn, or around 4:00 a.m., when he felt something or someone pushing against his side.

Drowsy and only half awake, he pushed back. "What's the matter, honey? Getting lonesome all by yourself?" He thought it was Dorothy pushing against him.

David reached back and grabbed a handful of fur. "What the hell!" he shouted and sat up. A huge black bear was standing on all fours between him and Dorothy.

The animal growled a low warning sound. David struck out instinctively, his fist landing on the bear's sensitive nose.

The bear stepped back and its hind feet became entangled with Dorothy and her sleeping bag. She screamed and the animal snarled and grabbed her by the right arm, high up near her shoulder. Its teeth sunk into soft flesh and bones cracked.

Dorothy screamed again: "David, help me! He's biting my arm."

158

David jumped up and reached over with both hands, grabbing the bear's fur near his powerful hindquarters. He pulled, shouted, and kicked at the 400-pound animal.

The bear suddenly dropped his biting hold on Dorothy's arm, turned, and struck with his front paw at David. The blow landed on David's hip, and extended claws ripped flesh to the bone.

The force of the blow smashed David back against the car. He could feel blood flowing from his wound.

The bear turned back to Dorothy and again took her arm in its mouth and began to drag her toward the edge of the woods.

Dorothy screamed, "The radio, David! The CB radio! Call for help."

David managed to get to his feet, open the car door, and switch on the CB radio. He grabbed the microphone. "Help! For God's sake, someone hear me and get to us with help."

A voice answered immediately. "This is ranger headquarters. What is your location and what is the problem?"

"We're at campground number twelve and my wife is being attacked by a bear. Please hurry. He's dragging her away."

"We're on our way. Switch on your headlights. It will help us find you and might frighten the bear away."

David reached over and switched the headlights on.

The bear had dragged Dorothy out of her sleeping bag and around in front of the car. When the light went on, it looked up, still holding her by the right arm close to her shoulder. It growled and shook its massive head.

David watched in horror as Dorothy's arm became detached from the rest of her body and a great fountain of blood spewed into the air.

The bear turned and ran toward the edge of the woods, still carrying Dorothy's arm in its mouth.

David ran to his wife. He thought she was unconscious, but when he had covered half the distance to her prone body, she sat straight up and screamed, "Jesus, save me. The bear is tearing my arm off. He'll kill me."

Before David could reach her she collapsed. When the rangers arrived only a few minutes later she was dead.

Carl Lehman, the chief park ranger in charge of camping facilities for the entire area, wrote in his report: "The man was covered with blood and was holding his wife's body in his arms. He was in a state of shock as a result of his own wound, which required 35 stitches to close it. We had to proceed quickly without regard to his wife, who was already dead. At the park emergency hospital they reported that had we been five minutes later in delivering David Pearlman to them he would not have survived."

Survival Techniques and Analysis

David and Dorothy Pearlman Case

This incident may seem out of character with the other cases covered in *Survival*. But actually it demonstrates an important part of the concept that *Survival* is trying to impart. Dangers have always threatened man's existence. He is among the weakest of all animals. He hasn't the ability to bite, claw, or run fast enough to escape being annihilated by animals bigger and stronger than he. Still he rules the land and all of its animals. Why? Because of his ability to think, to reason, to plan measures that will protect him against the attack of stronger beasts. The tragic night in Yellowstone Park demonstrates that when man neglects to use his weapon of reason and dares to challenge a brutal assailant on a one-to-one basis, he will in most cases lose. It makes no difference whether the assailant is a bear or another human being bent on killing. It makes no difference whether the location is Madison Avenue in New York City or a wilderness area in Yellowstone Park. The rules for survival remain the same: sensible protective measures, recognition of potential dangers, and careful planning which will deny the opportunity for tragic events to occur.

There are a number of simple measures that David and Dorothy might have taken to avoid that fatal attack. They had been warned before entering the park of the dangers of wild bears. Everyone hears a lecture given by the rangers before being allowed to enter the gates. From the beginning the Pearlmans ignored the warnings and proceeded as though no danger existed. Remember the frying pan filled with half-cooked food sitting on the flat sandstone rock. That was probably the lure that brought the bear to their campsite in the first place.

David was raised in the Colorado mountains and certainly knew better than to strike a 400-pound bear on its nose. It's true he was acting in fear and panic, but when David punched it the bear was not yet attacking anyone. It was the blow to its nose that caused the bear to attack. David's single act of blind panic caused the death of his wife. A primary lesson of *Survival*.

To have remained passive, absolutely still, would probably have saved Dorothy's life. The bear was hunting for food and would not ordinarily attack unprovoked. If left alone, it would probably have wandered off without doing harm.

In the Pearlman case the total defense was in prevention. Once the bear had started its attack, there was very little that either David or Dorothy could have done to stop it.

Bears are short-tempered creatures and once aroused are deadly.

Another element is that the Pearlmans were on vacation. The word *vacation* often connotes a relaxing of daily responsibilities which precludes the disciplined process of viewing potential dangers in a new environment.

For some strange reason, men and women in our society find caution and sensibleness while on vacation to be a restrictive harness or leash that will somehow deny them the opportunity of complete fulfillment. But how many thousands of vacations have been ruined by overexposure to the sun on some beautiful beach? How many hours wasted in bed or running back and forth to the bathroom because someone didn't think of the consequences of overeating and drinking? How many fun-filled vacations have ended in tragedy because vacationers overestimated their prowess as swimmers or did not consider the hazards of ocean swimming compared to their own private pools? All these things can be attributed to the lack of judgment that appears to infest the world of vacationers.

Another case I know of also occurred several years ago in Yellowstone Park. A man whom I shall call Larry Jones, with his wife, Eleanor, and two little girls age nine and five, had just finished listening to the ranger's talk about how to avoid trouble with the park's bear population. Jones, in his late thirties with no experience in wilderness areas, had listened with impatience to what he considered a childish scolding. He was an aggressive top executive in a large electronics company and resented being lectured to. As he and his family entered the park in their bright new Cadillac, he remarked, "No damned dumb bear is going to spoil my vacation. I won't bother them, and they had better not bother old Larry Jones or they'll get their tail twisted."

Eleanor and the children laughed. The nine-year-old reminded her father, "Daddy, bears don't have a tail long enough to twist. Just a short stubby thing."

Eleanor had packed a picnic lunch in a wicker basket, and about a mile inside the park they came upon a picnic ground with tables and benches.

Larry pulled over and stopped the car. "Here's a good spot for lunch. It's about another hour to our campgrounds and that's too long to wait. Eleanor—you bring the food basket. Come on kids; let's go."

It took only a few minutes to unpack their food and Eleanor spread it out on the tabletop. Larry started to build a fire in the stone fire pit and unwrapped a small aluminum frying pan. He was going to fry hamburger patties.

Suddenly one of the children hollered, "There's a bear and he's heading this way!"

Larry looked up. He saw a black bear waddling across the road heading toward them. "Eleanor—you and the children get back into the car," he called. "I'll take care of Mr. Bear if he comes snooping around."

Eleanor took the children and headed for the car. "Larry," she cautioned, "remember what the ranger said. Come get into the car until the bear leaves. If he takes the food, it's no great loss."

Larry waved to them. "Get in the car. No damned bear is going to eat my lunch."

The bear had arrived at the end of the table and was licking his chops. Everything on that tabletop looked good to him. As he reared up on his hind legs and put his 300 pounds on the edge of the table, it turned over, spilling the food on the ground.

Larry Jones, a smart electronics company executive, ran toward the 300-pound bear armed only with a small aluminum frying pan. When he got to the bear, Larry raised his frying pan and struck the animal a resounding blow on top of its huge head.

"Larry!" Eleanor screamed. "Larry! Be careful! You've got to be crazy."

Larry Jones never had a chance to answer. The bear hit him with its huge paw in the right side. The blow knocked Larry at least fifty feet, tearing him open and shattering ribs. Other vacationers in parked cars raced to the ranger's station. In five minutes an ambulance came and carted Larry off to the hospital. The bear, having disposed of Larry, enjoyed his lunch and ambled off.

Later in the hospital the rangers cited Larry for bothering the bear, and that citation cost him $150. The doctors sewed him back together using 180 stitches. Two weeks later he left the hospital, his vacation over, and headed back for home.

Readers of *Survival* should brand the initials VLOJ into their consciousness (they stand for "vacation lack of judgment") and make a resolve that it will never happen to them. In unfamiliar surroundings, judgment factors should be sharpened, not dulled.

20

Santa Monica, California, June 12, 1979. Betty and Joseph Ballentine drove north on 15th Street after making a left turn from Montana Avenue. It was 11:45 p.m. and a low fog created a curtain, forcing Joseph to drive very slowly as he and his wife approached their home in an affluent section of the beach city.

Betty, fifty-five years old and a beautiful blond former high-fashion model, smiled at her husband and her blue eyes sparkled. "What a wonderful evening, Joseph. The orchestra has never played better. You know, dear, our season tickets to Hollywood Bowl bring us our best entertainment. Dances, theaters, and the Dodgers are all fun, but the evenings at the Bowl are the best.

Joseph Ballentine, gray, tall, and slender, nodded. "I agree," he said quietly. "There's something about hearing that kind of music under the stars. It has the ability to transport one away from the heat and smog. It releases tensions I build up throughout the day hammering at a jury in a stuffy courtroom. Most important, it never tires me. Right now I feel wonderful. It's past our bedtime, but there is no feeling of fatigue." He swung the car into the small circular drive which was in front of their two-story Spanish-style home and switched off the ignition.

"Aren't you going to put the car away?" Betty asked, looking at her husband. Sometimes he did things that irritated her—leaving the car sitting out all night in the drive was one of those things. "Joseph, you shouldn't leave the car out. It only takes a minute to put it in the garage. I just don't understand why you dislike doing that."

Joseph stepped out and walked around the car to open the door for his wife. "Don't worry about it, dear. I've got to leave early in the morning and it is more convenient for me."

As Betty stepped out of the car, an old model Dodge, possibly a 1968 two-door, pulled up to the curb. It was occupied by four black men.

Betty grabbed Joseph's arm and froze. "What do they want?" she asked anxiously.

Before Joseph could answer, all four men piled out of the car and surrounded the startled couple.

Joseph held Betty close. "Take it easy, honey," he whispered.

The four strangers were all in their late teens or early twenties. Two of them displayed heavy revolvers and waved them close to Joseph's face. One, a short stocky man with a close-cropped beard, spoke up: "Everything you have in your pockets, mister. Put it all on the hood of your car." He turned to Betty. "Your purse, lady—put it there too, and the rings—all of them. That necklace"—he pointed to the four-strand gold choker Betty wore around her neck—"it too."

Betty and Joseph did what they were told. It all happened in seconds. One of the unarmed men scooped everything from the car's hood into a plastic bag and handed it to the fourth man, who took it back to the old Dodge and threw it into the back seat.

Joseph hoped they would leave. There was nothing more they could take. But they made no move to leave the scene.

The man who had flung the loot into the back seat of their car returned. He was tall and slender, clean-shaven with a moderate Afro hairstyle. All of the men were dressed in dirty slacks, tennis shoes, and loose flowing shirts. They had been drinking and Joseph, who as an attorney had handled many criminal cases involving drugs, recognized the anise-licorice odor of PCP.

The tall slender man walked by Joseph; as he came close to Betty, he suddenly turned and grabbed the front of her gown. With a single ripping motion he tore it from her shoulders, leaving bare breasts exposed. His voice was smooth and silky. "I want a piece of you, lady. Here or in the house."

The heavyset man holding his gun close to Joseph's head cautioned, "Not in the house. It's probably alarmed. Screw her right here. The grass will be a little wet, but she'll be under you."

The tall man tore Betty away from Joseph's arm. "Come on, lady," he purred. "You heard the man—it's going to be on the grass." He laughed. "A little ass on the grass. How does that grab you?"

Betty Ballentine was frightened, but she was not going to give in without a fight. She pulled free from the black man's grasp and struck at him with a clawed hand.

Blood streamed down his face as her nails raked his right cheek. "You dirty bitch," he screamed. He struck her hard and Betty fell to the ground.

Joseph shouted, "Leave her alone!" He took one step toward the tall man.

The heavyset man yanked him back and, placing the gun against Joseph's head, pulled the trigger. Joseph Ballentine died instantly.

It didn't end there. Betty saw her husband killed and screamed, "My God, why are you killing us?"

The tall man fell on top of her and, with savage aggressiveness, tore at her clothes and then raped her. When he finished, he stood up and said to the man who had killed Joseph, "Shoot her."

The man who held the second gun interrupted, "No. She's mine."

Five days later in St. John's Hospital, Betty Ballentine told how the man with the second gun had stood over her and fired twice. One bullet hit her in the belly and the other in her chest. Then the four men ran to their car and drove away. Neighbors who had been awakened by the shooting and screaming had come to Betty's aid, and fast medical assistance had saved her life. Betty Ballentine told police, "I could never have believed that human beings could act so cruelly."

Survival Techniques and Analysis

Betty and Joseph Ballentine Case

Betty Ballentine's last remark underscores one of the basic problems I've been trying to present in *Survival*. It is hard for anyone to believe that human beings can act with so little regard for the lives of others, to understand that in today's society such acts of vicious disregard for human life are becoming commonplace. Insofar as the public is concerned, there is little understanding of the effects of modern drugs—how they can turn a person into a raving killer, a destructive maniac without conscience, a rapist and a murderer. Joseph Ballentine had some knowledge of such occurrences but failed to apply them to himself. It was always the other person who was caught in these tragic acts. Because he never considered himself to be a part of such a scenario, when it happened he had no place to go.

The tragedy seems particularly frightening because it burst out of such a lovely evening. The location, an affluent section of a large city, the circumstances, a pleasurable night spent listening to the Los Angeles Philharmonic at the Hollywood Bowl—none of this strikes us as a backdrop for violent crime. But this may be the key to why Betty and Joseph—and so many others—blinded themselves with the "it can't happen to me" syndrome. We all tend to localize tragic and vicious acts of violence to equally sordid surroundings. In other words, we assume that if we keep our surroundings clean, acceptable, and idealistic, then none of the bad things will happen to us. That is not true. There is no way we can control those who participate in such violence. If we are targeted by them, it isn't going to make any difference how we conduct our personal lives. Those who will try to victimize us will not be deterred by the fact that we haven't spent an evening in some burlesque joint on Main Street. They don't give a damn where we have spent the evening; in fact, it is quite possible that such criminals will prey upon those who frequent the more expensive and culturally acceptable places.

I'm not going to say that our selection of living location, entertainment, and company will not have a bearing on our percentage chances of being attacked. Any one of those things can reduce the element of chance involved, but they are not reliable shields against our being victimized.

There are several courses of action Betty and Joseph Ballentine might have taken to avoid that murderous attack. One thing is certain: they should not have become so involved in the evening's entertainment, the process of driving home, their disagreement about putting the car in the garage, or anything else to the extent of forgetting their own position. It was late at night and they were well-dressed, affluent-looking people driving a reasonably expensive car. All of these conditions made them a logical target for prowling thieves. I doubt that either one of them gave any thought to their safety from the moment they left the Bowl until they were under attack in their own drive.

This raises an important point for all of us to keep in mind: *Know what's going on around you.* Recognize the presence and possibility of dangerous situations. The four men in that car had to have zeroed in on Joseph's car somewhere. They may have followed their victims all the way from the Bowl, picked them up between the Bowl and the Ballentine home—or they might have been waiting at Betty and Joseph's home or close by, just prowling and waiting for someone to show up. In any event, they weren't invisible. If Joseph or Betty had been reasonably cautious, they would have noticed the car with the four men in it. It was after midnight, there were few cars moving on the street where Betty and Joseph lived, and once they got close to their home they would probably have recognized anyone who belonged there. Even at the last moment when their assailants stopped at the curb, Betty was still in the car. Joseph could have gotten back in and driven away. The fact is, neither of them was thinking of their own safety until it was too late.

The best plan would have been to get back in the car and drive to the nearest police station. Which brings up another point. We should all know where the nearest police station is and the shortest route to it. I can guarantee you tbe four men would not have followed their intended victims into the police station. The Ballentines might have had to wait a few minutes, but I am sure the police would have escorted them home and seen them safely inside.

Still another circumstance makes the Ballentine case a needless tragedy and the result of careless indifference.

When they first drove into the driveway of their home, Betty suggested to Joseph that he put their car in the garage. In the glove compartment was an automatic garage door opener—one push of a button and they could have driven in and closed the door behind them. The garage was connected to the house with a door leading into the kitchen area. There would have been no reason for the Ballentines to have come out where they were vulnerable to attack.

I'll say it again: one of the major points that *Survival* strives to make is that a large amount of crime is made possible because of our propensity to create perfect opportunities for the criminal to strike. We can storm at the police, accuse the court systems, and scream our heads off for better protection: none of that will accomplish the goals we seek.

Law enforcement agencies are overburdened to the point where it is impossible for them to handle the growing crime situation. If we contemplate increasing those forces so they can meet the challenge, taxes will climb to a level we could not possibly afford. It is up to us to become involved in our own safety. We must began to deny opportunity by commonsense application of the programs set forth in *Survival*. If we all took such steps, the crimes in this country would drop to the point where our police agencies would have a chance to control those who seek to prey on others.

It is not valid to compare our police agencies with their counterparts in other countries. Other countries have different forms of government and different ideas about their police. But I can say this: our American police agencies are by far the best trained, administered, and devoted to their duty. No other law enforcement agency in the world can begin to match American agencies in these categories. Let me put it this way. You can rave, rant, and accuse your police department of every oppressive act in the book, but be sure of one thing—when you're in trouble and need help, they'll be there and, if necessary, will lay down their lives so that you and yours can live. "No man has greater love."

Epilogue

S URVIVAL IS NOT MEANT to be the sort of book that gets read and then put aside. My intent in writing *Survival* was that it be used—that its lessons be put into practice and its techniques be applied by people to any dangerous situations they might be forced to confront in their lives.

The scenarios I have presented all end in tragedy and violence—in many cases, with murder. Not one of them need have ended this way. Innocent blood shed, death, robbery, and sexual abuse could have been avoided if the victim had been prepared. Let's see what might have happened in one of the scenarios if the victims had been able to use the techniques of *Survival* in overcoming a potentially deadly situation.

The dogwoods were blossoming in this peaceful residential section of Atlanta, and Pat and Helen Connely were thankful to be spending a quiet Saturday morning at home. Tomorrow would be Helen Connely's 50th birthday. The preparations were all set: the Connelys would be joined by their three children and their spouses and five grandchildren for a big family-style dinner.

Pat Connely smiled to himself as he opened the hall closet where he had hidden a special surprise gift for his wife. Helen was busy tidying up their bedroom at the back of the house, and he knew she wouldn't be through for several minutes. But just to make sure, he called, "Need any help, Helen?"

"Heavens, no!" came the reply. "You'd think I know how to make up a bed after thirty-one years of marriage."

"Just checking," Pat said with a chuckle; then he took out the gift from the back of the closet and slipped his birthday card under the ribbon. He returned the gift to its hiding place behind some old golf bags and shut the closet.

Just then there came a loud knock on the front door.

Pat wondered who it could be at this hour of the morning. "Are you expecting visitors?" he called back to Helen.

"Must be some door-to-door salesman," she answered. "They always seem to come in the morning."

Pat walked up to the front door and asked, "Who's there?"

There was a moment's silence; then a man's voice said, "Parcel post. Package delivery."

The voice sounded OK, but Pat wanted to make sure. Parcel post usually delivered to his neighborhood in the afternoon. He put his eye up to the wide-angle peephole that he had installed the previous month and looked out. There, standing right on the orange circle he had painted on his slate porch for this very purpose, were two men wearing the uniforms of parcel post. They were Caucasians, in their thirties, both with longish blond hair. Nothing out of order, Pat decided, and he removed the heavy chain and opened the door.

Before Pat could say a word, the two men walked into his house and closed the door behind them. Pat knew at once he had made a mistake. He could tell from their faces—rough and scarred with bloodshot eyes—that, despite the uniforms, these two were not delivery men. "You said there was a package?" he demanded in a steady voice. "Where is it?"

174

The taller one, who had a broken nose, answered, "That was just a story, pops. We're not parcel post men." He took a small handgun from his pocket. "This should give you an idea of our business."

The second man moved quickly to grab Pat by the elbows. Pat noticed that he was unarmed and that his hands were trembling slightly.

"Get his pockets," the gunman ordered.

As the second man was roughly turning out the contents of his pockets, Pat heard his wife's footsteps coming down the hall. He spun his head rapidly and, the moment she came into view, gave two vigorous nods in her direction. Helen immediately raised her right hand to her right earlobe and tugged it. Then she turned and ran back down the hall. Pat heard a door slam and a heavy deadbolt lock fall into place. It all happened in seconds.

"What the hell was that?" the gunman shouted.

The second man shoved Pat hard in the chest. "Who's hiding back there?" he demanded in a high-pitched voice. "Tell us or we'll shoot you."

"That was my wife," Pat replied. "She saw you both and she's calling the police right now. You two better take what you want and get out of here fast."

"Yeah, we'll see about that," the gunman snorted. "Hey"—he turned to his partner—"tie this guy up and get him on the floor. I'm gonna go finish off the lady."

Helen Connely had been tipped off to the danger by the signals that she and her husband had devised together. Two nods of the head, the signal Pat had given her, meant go at once to the "safe harbor" and call the police; Helen signaled her understanding of and agreement with this course of action by tugging on her right earlobe.

The Connelys' safe harbor was in the back bathroom of the house. They had equipped the bathroom door with a sturdy deadbolt lock, installed a phone extension, and hooked up a panic button alarm system terminating in the house of their next-door neighbor.

The first thing Helen did after locking herself in the bathroom was to hit the panic button alarm. This would warn the neighbor there was trouble. Then, as she heard the heavy footsteps of the gunman come down the hall, she picked up the phone extension and called the police. The telephone number of the local police station was taped right to the phone, along with other emergency numbers.

Once she got the police on the phone, Helen gave her name, address, and brief descriptions of the two intruders. All the while she could hear doors crashing, rooms being ransacked, and loud voices outside. Then, as she set down the phone, Helen heard pounding on the bathroom door.

"OK, lady," the gunman yelled. "I know you're in there—so let's cut out the fun and games. You come on out or I blow your husband away!"

Helen remained silent. She and Pat had worked out in advance that, in the event of such an intrusion, the person in the safe harbor should say nothing to give him or herself away.

"Hey! Bring the old guy down here," the gunman shouted to his partner.

The second man, who had tied up Pat and put him on the floor of the front room while the gunman was searching the house for Helen, jerked him to his feet. "No funny stuff," he warned as he pushed Pat down the hall in front of him.

The gunman seized Pat by the arm when he came near and held the gun to his head. "OK, pops, tell your old lady to clear out of there."

Pat was careful to make no sudden movements. There was no sign of fear or panic in his voice as he said slowly and deliberately, "I won't do that. My wife has already seen you, so she's a witness to your crime. There's nothing you can do about that. You two had better just try to get away while you still can."

"Witness, huh?" the gunman said. "Then I guess I'll just have to waste the both of yous."

He acted as if he were about to pull the trigger, but Pat spoke up again, still in a calm, reasonable tone. "Think about it first. If you kill me now and my wife escapes, you'll be convicted of murder for sure. But if you leave right now—what do they have on you? Almost nothing. You might not even go to jail at all. Take what you can find here and get out."

"Maybe the old bastard's right," the second man blurted out. "These two got too many tricks up their sleeves. I've had it."

"You shut up and stay where you are," his partner ordered. "Can't you tell a bluff when you hear one?" He turned back to the bathroom door. "This is it, lady," he shouted, "your last chance." He paused and then fired two bullets at the lock. Something seemed to give way. The gunman raised his right leg and kicked the bathroom door as hard as he could. It burst open.

Inside the bathroom, Helen Connely was prepared. The moment she had a clear view, she aimed her revolver and fired. A bullet lodged neatly in the gunman's right shoulder, forcing him to lower his arm with the gun. Pat Connely had, by prearranged plan, dropped to the floor so that he was out of range when the firing started.

The gunman's partner swore under his breath and fled back down the hall. The gunman, now clutching his wounded shoulder, followed seconds later. In the distance could be heard the rising and falling wail of police sirens. The two intruders stumbled out of the Connelys' house and into the arms of the law.

Helen Connely had a lot to celebrate the next day on her 50th birthday. Most of all, she and her husband had survived.